40 DIGITAL
SLR
TECHNIQUES

Y.

ISBN: 981-05-3520-1

Printed in the Republic of Korea.

How to contact us:

support@youngjin.com
feedback@youngjin.com.sg
Fax: 65-6339-1403

Credits

Authors: Darrell Tan, Eu Lee
Production Editor: Patrick Cunningham
Editor: Bill Cassel
Indexer: Lee Sang-hun
Book and Cover Design: Litmus

A Note from the Author

Today, in both amateur and professional photography, the digital SLR has arrived. We now have equipment that can produce image quality rivaling and even exceeding that of 35mm film. Even as performance has improved, so prices have fallen, offering everyone something that suits their budget.

If you intend to buy a digital SLR (DSLR), or have already done so, this book is for you. You may be experienced with film SLRs, but new to digital capture (as I was); or you may be upgrading from a compact digital camera. You might even be new to photography. My goal is to offer you clear and practical know-how so that you can make quick progress.

The "digital" and "SLR" characteristics of a DSLR both warrant a proper orientation. The first part of this book deals with the camera itself, plus lenses and accessories.

The next portion of the book covers basic techniques for shooting in some common situations. You'll learn some guidelines for approaching different subjects, and using your camera skillfully.

Digital photography doesn't end when you take a photo. You'll want to store and share your photos, possibly enhancing them as well. Knowing that some may find computers daunting, I've tried to introduce all this as simply as I can in the concluding chapters.

I hope that in reading this book, you'll gain essential skills and knowledge, and be rewarded with greater pleasure in your photography.

Darrell Tan

C o n t e n t s

40 Digital SLR Techniques

Understanding Digital SLRs

Digital SLR cameras are becoming increasingly popular because their designs blend the features of 35mm film SLRs with the imaging wizardry of the latest digital cameras. This allows for professional-level cameras that are comfortable to use, sturdy, and have the capability to capture startling images under a wide range of conditions and situations.

To understand DSLRs, let's first look at how these cameras function. This chapter will outline some common, basic features. If you're still shopping for a camera, this will aid your search. If not, consider this a primer for the camera you already own. We will also look at basic accessorizing and care, then spend some time discussing the digital sensor and image processing.

The following chapter will provide a solid foundation for understanding DSLRs. It will also place in context the 40 techniques found in this book, and pave the way for your mastery of digital photography.

I Comparing DSLRs to Other Cameras

A digital single-lens reflex camera, or DSLR, is an advanced photographic tool. If you put in some time to understand what it is and what it can do, you will be rewarded with superb results. If you are moving from a consumer or prosumer digital camera to a DSLR, the difference in construction, the use of interchangeable lenses, and the large number of accessories are the main benefits. If you are moving from a film SLR to a digital SLR, the use of a digital sensor (and memory card) in place of film is the main advantage.

Single-Lens Reflex System

A single-lens reflex (SLR) camera provides both reflex viewing and image capture using just one lens situated in front of the sensor. Reflex viewing uses a system of prisms and/or mirrors to direct the image from the rear of the lens to the viewfinder. This enables the photographer to view exactly what the lens sees—a crucial feature when composing photos, because it ensures that what you see is what you'll get. When the photograph is taken, the mirror in front of the sensor flips out of the way and the image is transmitted to the sensor (rather than the viewfinder).

▲ A DSLR allows viewing through the lens itself.

▲ This compact digital camera has a viewfinder separate from the lens.

Differences between DSLRs and Digital Compact or Prosumer Cameras

DSLR	Compact or Prosumer
Optical reflex viewfinder shows what the lens sees with great clarity. There is no parallax error.	Separate optical viewfinders have parallax error. Electronic (LCD) viewfinders have no parallax error but provide a poor view. Some LCD models have no viewfinder, using the main LCD screen for composing and reviewing shots.
Viewfinder enables intermittent viewing and tracking of subject in-between shots during continuous shooting.	Electronic viewfinders and LCD screens usually black out in continuous shooting mode.
Viewfinder image is about as bright as the actual scene.	Most LCD viewfinders or screens can increase or decrease their brightness, for easier viewing.
Almost all DSLRs use the LCD screen only for reviewing captured images (due to the reflex viewing system).	LCD screen can be used to preview images before capture as well as review captured images.
Cannot record movies (also due to the reflex system), though some allow audio annotation of images.	Can record movies and/or audio.
Larger pixel size (about 100-180 pixels/mm) helps lower noise (random specks) and allows higher ISO settings (up to 1600 is common).	Small sensors require smaller pixel sizes (about 280-450 pixels/mm), increasing image noise and limiting ISO range (usually to 400 or 800 maximum).
Mechanical parts—shutter, mirror, lens mount—result in greater bulk and battery consumption; lenses have to be larger to provide image for larger sensors (though zooming is manual).	Less bulk due to all-in-one construction, smaller sensor, and lens sizes (lens zooming consumes power, however).
Mirror causes noise and vibration in the camera body when shutter is released.	Shooting is relatively quiet and discreet; no additional vibration caused.
Image shape usually follows 35mm film (3:2 ratio).	Image shape follows most computer monitors (4:3 ratio).
Lenses are interchangeable, with wide variation in cost and performance.	Lenses are non-interchangeable, though conversion lenses are available for some cameras.
Dust can enter through the lens mount and dirty the sensor.	Sensor is sealed and not prone to contamination.
Images may seem soft and too dark when viewed on a computer, but this is to allow for image manipulation using software.	Images tend to look sharp and have vivid color right out of the camera, ready for printing/sharing.

Differences between DSLRs and Film SLRs

DSLR	Film SLR
Start-up varies from instant to a few seconds.	Instantaneous start-up.
Can capture hundreds of images without changing memory card (depending on camera settings and card type). Images can be deleted to free up space.	12, 24, or 36 images captured per roll of film before reloading is required (unless special bulk film adapter is used).
Images can be reviewed quickly.	No way to view images before film is developed.
Battery charge can last for several hundred shots; cannot operate without batteries.	Batteries can last for thousands of shots (depending on model and conditions). Mechanical models may operate without batteries.
Viewfinder image is usually smaller, as digital sensors are usually smaller than a 35mm film frame.	Large viewfinder image.
Smaller sensor sizes change lenses' effective field of view with respect to film.	36mm × 24mm film frame standard for all SLRs.
Easy conversion from color to black-and-white, but some images may not have the "feel" of film.	Only one film type usable at a time, though some films have "classic" qualities, such as color or contrast.
White balance can be set without correction filters.	Requires filters or flash to correct color temperature.
Lenses for film SLRs may be used, though some DSLRs use digital-only lenses designed for smaller sensors.	Cannot use lenses designed solely for DSLRs.
Images not harmed by X-rays and can be duplicated and archived without any quality loss.	Undeveloped film vulnerable to X-rays. Developed film originals must be carefully stored.

Sensors, Processors, and Image Files

The imaging system is the heart of any DSLR. (It is a testament to the engineering skills of designers that DSLR images can equal film quality.) Knowledge of how this system works will help you get the most out of your camera.

The main components involved in image recording and processing are the image sensor and the image processor. The following section will introduce their basic functions. We'll also introduce the parameters that affect image files.

Image Sensor

Color film relies on layers that capture different wavelengths of light. In digital photography, color is recorded and expressed as a combination of red, green, and blue (RGB) values. Digital sensors comprise millions of pixels, which are microscopic (5-10μm across) light-sensing points; each pixel only captures one color value: red, green, or blue. Most DSLRs use CCD or CMOS sensors with square pixels arranged in the common Bayer pattern. Fujifilm's Super CCD sensors use octagonal pixels in two different sizes on a diamond-shaped grid. Foveon sensors are different: they have three stacked layers of pixels, each pixel position capturing all three colors.

The diagram below compares Bayer pattern sensors (left) to Foveon sensors (right).

▶ ▶ ▶ Analog-to-Digital Conversion and Interpolation

The sensor pixels generate electrical signals when light from the lens reaches them. These signals are converted into digital values by an analog-to-digital converter (ADC).

Since one pixel records only one color value, the value from each pixel and those of its immediate neighbors are interpolated by computation to determine the combined RGB value of each pixel point. For Foveon sensors, each pixel location has three superimposed pixels, so no color interpolation is needed.

▶ ▶ ▶ Sensor Shape

Most DSLR sensors, though they may differ in size, have an aspect ratio of 3:2 (or 1.5:1). This is the same ratio as the 35mm film SLRs they are based on (with a film frame of 36mm × 24mm). DSLRs based on the Four Thirds system, however, have an aspect ratio of 4:3 (about 1.33:1), the same ratio as digital compacts and standard computer monitors. The few DSLRs based on medium-format systems typically have aspect ratios based on their film counterparts.

▶ ▶ ▶ Sensor Resolution

Sensor resolution is calculated by multiplying the number of pixels along the width and height of the sensor. For example, a sensor measuring 3000 × 2000 pixels has a total of 6 million pixels (megapixels). Top-end DSLRs based on 35mm models have well in excess of 10 megapixels. Cameras based on medium-format systems may exceed 20 megapixels.

Sensor resolution divided by output resolution tells you how much you can enlarge the digital image. For a camera with 3000 × 2000 pixels, printing at an output resolution of 200 ppi (pixels per inch) would allow print dimensions of 15 × 10 inches. Printing at 300 ppi, however, would only allow a print of around 10 × 6.7 inches. More pixels means larger possible prints. Though you can enlarge images using computer software, this will impact the quality of the image. For this reason, the megapixel rating of your camera is critical.

Image Processor

All DSLRs use digital processing to adjust the digital signals from the sensor and ADC. Adjustments need to be made to white balance (to neutralize color cast), contrast, saturation, sharpening, noise reduction, and so on to produce the final image file. These steps are as important as the sensor itself in determining image quality. Cameras that allow custom settings for these processing parameters will allow you maximum control over the image creation process.

Image File Characteristics

After processing, each digital image is stored to memory as a computer-readable file. Additional processing may take place before storage, depending on your camera and settings.

▶ ▶ ▶ File Compression

To save memory space, digital files may be compressed. There are two main kinds of compression: lossless compression, which makes files smaller without losing any image information; and lossy compression, which saves more space by discarding some of the image data (and reducing image quality).

▶ ▶ ▶ Bit Depth

In digital images, gradations from brightest to darkest tones are not infinite. There are a limited number of brightness levels per color channel. The bit depth of the image file controls this. Each bit increment represents a doubling of possible values, so a bit depth of 1 allows two possible values (dark or light), and a bit depth of 2 allows four possible values (two additional intermediate levels). 8-bit images allow 256 levels per color channel and 12 bits allow 4096 levels per channel.

The greater the bit depth, the subtler tonal variations can be. To most viewers, however, 8-bit images are good enough to appear smooth (without visible transitions). This makes more sense when you realize that three color channels (RGB) with 8 bits each add up to a total of 24 bits of information, resulting in around 16.7 million different possible values per pixel!

Most DSLRs can capture more than 8 bits of information. They use the "extra" bit depth to generate higher quality 8-bit images.

▶ ▶ ▶ File Formats

DSLRs usually offer one or more of the following file formats for saving images:

● **JPEG**: This is a lossy compression format. It can be applied in different amounts, allowing the user to determine which is more important: file size or image quality. Most cameras offer two or three JPEG quality settings. Standard JPEG images are 8-bit.

● **TIFF**: This is a lossless format that can be either compressed or uncompressed. Only some digital cameras have this as an option. TIFF files take up more space, but allow for higher quality output. They can have more than 8 bits per channel. TIFF is losing popularity to RAW as an in-camera file format.

● **RAW**: This is not a universal file format, but refers to the "raw" sensor data received by the camera, before any processing is applied. The sensor data and processing parameters are saved in the camera maker's RAW file format. This way, any of these parameters (such as white balance) may be changed and re-applied to the raw data after capture, as if the photograph were being taken anew. RAW files are generally lossless, may be compressed or uncompressed, and also have high bit depth (commonly 12 or 14). They must be processed on a computer before conversion to other formats or printer output. Some DSLRs have a RAW+JPEG capture mode, which saves the unprocessed raw data and a processed JPEG of the same image at one go. See Chapter 6 for RAW techniques.

III Basic Functions and Considerations

A DSLR camera offers a wide range of functions and features, enabling it to be used for many types of photography. As you read through this section, refer to your camera manual to learn exactly what settings are available on your camera.

Lenses and Aperture

One of the major benefits of a DSLR is the ability to choose from a wide range of interchangeable lenses. Your camera may even come as a kit with one or more lenses. Note that each camera manufacturer uses a specific lens mount, which is the steel ring where lenses attach to the camera. You may use lenses from the camera manufacturer, or from third-party lens manufacturers who produce lenses that use the correct mount. Lenses with incompatible lens mounts won't attach and cannot be used unless a special adapter is available.

Since lenses are detachable, focal length and aperture will depend on the lens used. See the next section for further information.

▲ Nikon cameras use the Nikon F Mount for lenses.

Shutter Speed Range

DSLRs offer a range of shutter speeds that determine how long the shutter opens to let the sensor receive light. Conventionally, a plain number value represents a speed in fractions of a second (60 stands for 1/60th of a second). Therefore, a higher number means a faster shutter speed. Fast speeds are useful for stopping motion in a picture, such as in sports photography, or when capturing a very bright scene. On the other side of the equation, speed values that feature quotation marks indicate seconds (3" is 3 seconds); a higher number in these instances indicates a slower speed. "Bulb" mode is for exposures manually timed by the user. Exposures may be as long as battery life allows. Slow speeds are useful in dim situations, for photos showing motion, and to smoothen flowing water in a picture.

▲ A fast shutter speed freezes the motion of water droplets.

▲ A slow shutter speed turns the lights into swirls.

AF Performance and Low-Light Focusing

To bring a subject into sharp focus, DSLRs have one or more autofocus (AF) sensors. Cross-type AF sensors are more sensitive than linear ones. One or both types may be found on a camera, typically a cross-type in the center flanked by linear sensors. Users can usually choose whether one or more sensors are active.

DSLRs focus on the image seen through the lens, as compared to some compact digital cameras, which measure reflected infrared pulses to determine subject distance. The "passive" system used by DSLRs makes it possible to focus on reflections, through glass, and at long distances, where emitted beams (i.e., "active" AF) may be limited. Passive AF sensors may find it difficult to focus, however, when there is low contrast or very fine detail in the scene. Low contrast may be due to the lack of clear outlines or dim lighting. For the latter problem, some DSLRs can emit illuminating beams (either from the camera body or an attached external flash) to help the camera focus. These beams can be intrusive, though, so some users turn this AF-assist light off. When autofocus is not working well, it is often best to switch the camera to manual focus and turn the focus barrel until the subject appears the sharpest in the viewfinder. Some cameras will help you focus manually by giving you a signal in the viewfinder when you have focused correctly.

Frames per Second

In continuous shooting mode, the camera takes photos repeatedly as long as you depress the shutter button. The maximum rate of capture is given in frames per second (fps). DSLRs generally have a rapid frame rate. Still, captured images take time to be processed and stored. To allow photos to be taken rapidly, a buffer or temporary memory space is built into the camera. The buffer holds data which is waiting to be processed and stored. The maximum shooting rate can be maintained only until the built-in buffer is full; the camera can take another shot only when enough space has been cleared in the buffer. If you shoot in continuous mode, be aware of how many shots you can take in one burst.

ISO Range and Noise

ISO is a standard for measuring film speed; higher ISO values indicate greater sensitivity to light, which translates to faster exposure time. Unlike traditional SLRs, for which individual films have different ISO ratings, DSLRs allow you to change ISO at any time. When ISO is increased, the DSLR amplifies the sensor signals during image processing so that the sensor appears to have higher sensitivity to light. This allows you to use faster shutter speeds and/or smaller apertures in low light.

DSLR sensors usually provide crisp detail and smooth areas of tone from ISO settings of 100 to 400, depending on the camera model. Higher settings (such as 800), however, can result in the appearance of small spots of dark or random colors, akin to film grain, called "noise." Noise will be especially visible in shadowy areas. Of course, film of equivalent ISO also has noticeable grain, so this is to be expected. Noise can be reduced with computer software, although some image sharpness can be lost in the process.

Flash

High-end professional DSLRs do not have a built-in flash unit. The rest usually have a small pop-up flash on top of the camera body. A built-in flash is useful for lighting nearby subjects or for fill-in flash (described later in Chapter 2). For greater power, however, all DSLRs accept hotshoe-mounted external flash units. Although hotshoes are the same shape, each camera manufacturer has its own pattern of flash contacts, which are the tiny metal bits providing communication between the camera and flash unit. Since using the wrong flash can seriously damage your equipment's electronic circuitry, only use compatible flash units from the camera manufacturer or verified third-party vendors. DSLRs may also be used with studio strobes, though some may need a hotshoe adapter to trigger the studio flash.

▲ Hotshoe flash contacts

Flash sync speeds (i.e., the fastest shutter speed that can be used with flash) vary between cameras. Additionally, some cameras, when used with certain flashgun models which fire rapid bursts, can give very high sync speeds (though this method may decrease flash range). Higher sync speeds are generally required when using fill-in flash in bright daylight, or when background detail needs to be excluded.

Memory Card Formats

With the image resolution of today's DSLRs, large-capacity memory cards are needed to store captured images. Cards of one gigabyte (GB) and up are commonly used for the storage of a day's busy shooting, whether JPEG or RAW files. Some photographers prefer having several smaller cards, in case of card failure; others prefer having fewer, larger cards to reduce the need to change storage media.

Many DSLRs use CompactFlash (CF) or Microdrive cards. CF cards are solid-state (meaning they have no moving parts), while Microdrives contain a miniature hard disk. Both offer good price-storage value, although Microdrives are not designed to operate above 3000m altitude (where atmospheric pressure is low).

Some models have been designed with dual slots to allow for both CF/Microdrive and another smaller format, such as Secure Digital (SD). Some newer and smaller DSLRs only accept SD cards. The smaller media have the advantage of being compact, but maximum card capacities may trail behind those of the larger formats.

▲ CF and SD memory cards

Introduction

Memory cards in the same format are not all created equal. Different versions are produced with varying read and write speeds. Faster cards command a higher price for the same storage capacity. Generally, a fast card is recommended for DSLRs, but the rate of data transfer depends on the card as well as the camera. The system cannot operate faster than the slower of the two.

Battery Specifications

Many DSLRs utilize proprietary lithium batteries, which are rechargeable and relatively lightweight. They are supposed to have no "memory effect," meaning that they may be recharged before being fully discharged without ill effect. However, they can be rather expensive.

▲ Nikon Li-Ion battery and charger

▲ Sanyo NiMH AA batteries and charger

Some cameras make use of AA batteries. In this case, third-party rechargeable nickel metal hydride (NiMH) batteries are recommended for price and performance. They are available in different capacities, measured in mAh (milliamp hours). Higher-capacity batteries will power your camera longer. Although disposable cells may be used, alkaline batteries fall to an unusable voltage too quickly (though they may still be used for other devices).

To maximize battery life, minimize use of the LCD screen and other functions, such as autofocus and metering. If one set of batteries proves insufficient for your shooting needs, consider buying spare rechargeables and using them in rotation. Alternatively, some cameras can use add-on battery grips or belt-packs to supply even more power.

Anti-Shake Function

Some camera makers offer anti-shake, or image stabilization, as a feature. Some provide stabilizing elements in the lens to counter minor movements or vibrations. Stabilization can also be handled in the camera body. Konica Minolta DSLRs provide stabilization for the imaging sensor itself, so that anti-shake is available regardless of which lens is used. Image stabilization may allow you to use shutter speeds up to 8 times longer (3 stops slower) than for normal handheld shooting. Remember, though, that anti-shake mechanisms should be turned off when using a tripod.

Weather Seals and Build Quality

The toughest DSLRs use various metals for their internal frame and outer shell. They may also be sealed against dust and moisture. Low-end models may use plastics in their construction, but are robust enough for general use—not abuse! In any case, since every DSLR contains precision electronics and optics, avoid unnecessary impact or shock to your equipment. Also avoid dust, heat, moisture, salt spray, and chemicals that may affect the plastic or rubber parts of the camera.

Size and Weight

While they are similar in size and weight to comparable film SLRs, DSLRs are bulkier and heavier than standard digital prosumer cameras. This is because the sensor size, lens mount, mirror box, and prism are all inherited from 35mm SLR systems. So the potential to "miniaturize" DSLRs is limited.

The ideal camera size depends on the user's personal preference. While a small camera may be used quickly and unobtrusively, a larger body provides good counterbalance for the larger lenses that can be fitted to DSLRs. A hand grip that is too small can be tiring to hold compared to a larger one. Of course, too much weight can discourage you from taking your camera along, and that would defeat the entire purpose! The best way to go would be to try out different models to get a feel for what suits you best.

▲ A larger hand grip allows a comfortable hold for large lenses.

Lenses that only have one focal length are called prime, or fixed, lenses. Lenses with variable focal length are known as zoom lenses. Due to optical design and construction, prime lenses tend to deliver good image quality. Zoom lenses vary from professional quality to mediocre. Also, the greater the zoom range, the harder it is to maintain consistent image quality. Dividing the longest focal length by the shortest gives the zoom range. For example, an 18-55mm lens has a zoom range of 3 times, or 3x.

▶ ▶ ▶ Aperture

Aperture relates to the amount of light that passes through the lens to the camera sensor. This value is also called the f-stop, and is usually prefixed with an f (e.g., f/11; alternatively, f11 or 1:11). A smaller aperture has a larger number (e.g., f/16) and lets in less light, but has greater depth of field (DOF). A larger aperture has a smaller number (e.g., f/2.8) and lets in more light, though with less DOF.

Note: Aperture is technically a fraction, where f refers to the lens' focal length. Mathematically, f/16 is smaller than f/2.8. But it is common to compare the denominators and say that 16 is "larger" than 2.8.

Lenses with larger apertures are more costly to manufacture and more difficult to design. This is especially true of lenses of extreme focal lengths (e.g., 600mm). Larger apertures are sought after when there is a need for higher shutter speeds, reduced DOF, or lower ISO (these concepts are covered in depth later in the book). With zoom lenses, it is also more difficult to maintain the same aperture over the whole focal length range. Consequently, many zooms have reduced aperture at longer focal lengths. Those with constant aperture are more expensive.

A lens is therefore described by its focal length and maximum aperture. Prime lenses have one value for each aspect; a 50mm f/1.8 lens (sometimes abbreviated to 50/1.8), for example. Zoom lenses are described by minimum and maximum focal lengths, and maximum aperture (which may vary). Examples are 24-70mm f/2.8 (constant maximum aperture) and 28-80mm f/3.5-5.6 (the maximum aperture is f/3.5 at 28mm, decreasing to f/5.6 at 80mm).

▲ Two prime lenses, 24mm f/2.8 and 50mm f/1.8

▲ A zoom lens, with specifications of 18-70mm f/3.5-4.5

▶ ▶ ▶ Buying Lenses

Generally, with lenses you get what you pay for. A good rule of thumb is to buy only the lenses you need, and maximize their use. Only specialized fields of photography require the extreme short or long focal length lenses. A teleconverter (an attachment that works with a lens to multiply its focal length) is an economical option for those who need to lengthen their optical reach. Even if you do require a certain special focal length, ask yourself if you really need a model with a larger aperture. Most lenses perform well when used at their optimum aperture (f/8-11 is common). Chapter 2 explains lens types in further detail.

External Flash Units

A flash adds extra light and raises contrast for scenes that are too dark. Flash is also effective when shutter speeds are too slow for the camera to be held steady. A flash also lightens or fills in unwanted shadows caused by directional lighting. Additionally, a flash can be used as a more consistent source of light when ambient light is inconsistent.

The power of a flash unit is indicated by its guide number. This number is relative to a stated ISO, and is measured in meters or feet. For example, a flash may be rated GN32 (in meters) at ISO 100. When the guide number is divided by the lens aperture used, this gives the maximum flash reach. For example, using the above flash (with ISO 100) with an aperture of f/4 would yield a maximum flash range of 8m.

Flash units also vary in their degree of automation. You may want to look for a flash unit that allows through-the-lens (TTL) flash metering, which means that the DSLR will automatically control the flash output for best results. Some flashguns have a photo-electric sensor whereby they control their own output, but this is a more primitive method (though it can be effective).

▲ Flash unit attached to DSLR ▲ Flash head showing tilt and swivel

The most versatile flash units have heads which can tilt up and down, and swivel left and right. This will allow you to bounce the light from the flash off a ceiling or wall for a softer lighting effect. Some models can emit AF-assist beams, and a few can be triggered remotely by a burst from another flash unit. We'll cover flash features in greater depth later in the book.

Tripods

While the equipment described above is mainly produced by camera manufacturers, tripods are the domain of specialist third-party companies, such as Manfrotto and Gitzo. Almost all cameras use the standard 1/4" screw tripod mount, so the options are theoretically very wide. In reality, however, DSLR users have to be quite particular in this area as there are few real bargains in the tripod world.

The main purpose of a tripod is to keep the camera steady while the photo is taken. This can be as long as several seconds in some situations. A tripod needs to be sturdy and rigid enough to hold the camera and lens firmly despite their substantial combined weight (and the occasional breeze). Adjustment of camera position should be quick, precise, and sure, rather than slow and jerky. When you hold the camera to focus or take a picture, it should not quiver. Unfortunately, many smaller "travel" tripods do not meet these criteria.

Supposing that the tripod is sturdy and can support the load, another factor to consider is the maximum and minimum heights of the tripod. The tripod should be able to extend high enough so you will not have to crouch uncomfortably. You should also be able to set it up low enough if you require a low viewpoint.

Today's tripod legs can be made of aluminum, steel, or carbon fiber. They may consist of 3 or 4 leg extensions, secured by either clip or twist locks. On top, ball-head tripods allow instant adjustment in all three dimensions, while three-way heads allow individual control of the three dimensions of movement.

▶ Manfrotto tripods with ball head (left) and three-way head (right)

Many photographers find quick-release plates useful. These screw into the camera base. A camera with a plate attached can be mounted or removed from the tripod head very quickly and easily. As long as the whole system holds the camera firmly, quick-release plates can speed up your work. Try to look for designs that do not require the use of a coin to rotate the plate screw, as this can be rather inconvenient.

Card Readers

Though DSLRs can be linked directly to your computer to transfer images, you might prefer to use a memory card reader. There are two primary reasons for this. One is to save the camera batteries, and the other is to provide a higher transfer rate than the camera can give. Cameras with FireWire or USB 2.0 High Speed connections transfer at the fastest available speeds. Those with only USB 1.1 or 2.0 Full Speed connections, though, will benefit from a faster card reader interface. See Chapter 5 for more info on transfer and storage options.

▲ This USB 2.0 High Speed card reader allows for fast data transfer.

Computers and Software

Besides providing a hard disk for storing your images, a computer can come in handy for other purposes related to DSLR usage. A good selection of computer software for both Windows and Mac operating systems is available to photographers wishing to manipulate their images. Note that a fast processor and plenty of hard disk space and RAM will save time when working with images and image-related software.

Camera manufacturers offer proprietary software that can be used to adjust camera settings and even operate their cameras remotely from your computer. Images can be viewed on-screen immediately after capture.

Image editing software allows photos to be enhanced and tailored for various output devices. Proprietary software and some third-party software can process and convert RAW files. The industry standard is Adobe Photoshop, and this is discussed in Chapters 6 and 7.

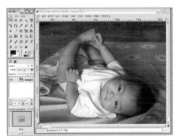

▲ The GIMP (http://www.gimp.org) is a free, powerful image editing program.

▲ Picasa (http://picasa.google.com) helps you manage and edit your collections of photos.

With images proliferating on your hard disk, an image management program will come in handy. Effective programs allow key words or phrases to be attached to your pictures, so that you can search for them more easily in the future.

Camera Care

As a tool for your photography, a DSLR will probably find itself exposed to various environmental conditions. Reasonable care and maintenance are required to keep it in good working order. The most important parts are those that are involved with the path of light rays: the lens and the sensor. These affect the quality of image capture and therefore warrant special attention.

If the cleaning methods described here are not effective, avoid using stronger or more abrasive techniques. Send your camera for professional cleaning or servicing instead.

Camera Body Care

The camera body should be dusted off with a dry, lint-free cloth or with a blower brush. If the camera has been exposed to salt spray or taken to the beach, you should use a very lightly dampened cloth to wipe the exterior, followed by a dry cloth, as soon as possible. Air the camera thoroughly afterwards.

Should the camera ever be splashed with water or dropped into the water, quickly turn the power off and remove the batteries. Dry the camera exterior as well as possible, especially the controls, dials, and hinges where water has entered. Open all doors and flaps, and leave the camera under a fan or in an air-conditioned environment until you are able to send the camera for servicing.

Inside the lens mount, you should be very cautious. Avoid changing lenses in wet or dusty environments so that foreign particles have less chance of entering. Regardless of your efforts, you may find dust on the mirror when you remove the lens. With a blower or soft brush, blow on or brush the mirror lightly to dislodge particles. Avoid touching or wiping the mirror or the viewfinder screen above it as they are very easily scratched. Point the lens mount downwards so particles fall out. Store the camera with a body cap if it is left without a lens attached.

The viewfinder eyepiece and the LCD screen are very delicate and should also be cleaned with care. Gently clean using a blower brush, lens tissue, or microfiber cloth.

ᴸens Cleaning

The surface of the lens facing your subject is the front element. The surface facing the lens mount is the rear element. These are the most vulnerable parts of the lens and you should avoid touching them. Modern lens glass is multicoated, and excessive cleaning can easily scratch or even remove the necessary multicoating. Use a UV filter, available from camera stores, to protect the front element. If dirt or fingerprints do get onto the lens, use the following methods to gently clean it.

- Use a blower bulb to blow loose particles off the glass.
- A soft brush can be used to dislodge dust specks.
- Instead of a brush, you can also use lens cleaning tissue. One method is to roll a piece up, then tear it in two. The torn surface will work like a brush.
- A microfiber cloth can be used to clean water spots or fingerprints off the lens. Lightly wipe the lens in a circular motion. Alternatively, you may use lens cleaning tissue with a little lens cleaning fluid. Always put a drop or two of the fluid on the tissue and never directly on the lens.

Sensor Cleaning

The image sensor in a DSLR is covered by a thin and very easily damaged glass filter. No matter how careful you are, dust particles will inevitably find their way onto it, through the lens mount. Dirt must be removed or it will cause specks in every photo you shoot.

First, try non-contact cleaning. If you own an Olympus DSLR, the camera's Supersonic Wave Filter function should do the job. Otherwise, use a clean blower bulb; a dirty bulb may blow out tiny specks trapped inside it. Hold the camera with the lens mount facing down and insert the fine end of the blower, ensuring that the tip does not touch the sensor. If several strong puffs do not dislodge and remove the dirt, you'll need to take further action.

Contact cleaning of a sensor requires special equipment, consisting of a flexible wiper, clean-room quality swabs, and residue-free cleaning liquid. You can get these items from photography suppliers. Follow the included instructions closely. Generally, the goal is to pass a swab moistened with cleaning fluid over the sensor, without using the same portion of swab twice. If this sounds too risky to you, send the camera for professional cleaning instead.

Dry Box

Multicoated surfaces are susceptible to fungal growth in humid environments. Fungus may grow on the external and internal glass surfaces of a lens and has the appearance of fine feathery lines. If this occurs, the transmission of light through the lens may be affected, and the multicoated layers can also be permanently damaged. Such lenses must be sent for professional cleaning as they may have to be disassembled. To prevent this, keep your camera body and lenses in a low-humidity environment. One way is to use a dry box, which can be adjusted to maintain the internal humidity at 45-55%.

▲ Dry boxes are available in different sizes.

▲ A small, battery-operated hygrometer

To monitor the humidity level inside the box, you can put in a hygrometer. Alternatively, you can store your equipment in any airtight container, using silica gel to absorb moisture. Silica gel can be heated to remove absorbed moisture, then reused.

Camera Bags and Cases

A bag will protect equipment from day-to-day hard knocks plus strong vibrations, dust, and water.

For urban environments, a soft bag may be all that is required. Ensure that other hard objects, such as keys, do not rub or scratch your equipment. If carrying additional lenses or accessories, put them in pouches or even clean socks to separate them.

For greater protection, use a purpose-built camera bag. These are available in numerous sizes and configurations. Some accept add-on pouches and straps. Backpack designs are useful for even distribution of weight, especially important with heavy equipment or on long walks. Shoulder-slung designs are better for access to equipment or keeping your eye on your camera kit.

▲ A shoulder bag gives you easy access to your camera.

Some bags have a water-resistant coating under the material for protection against inclement weather. Others have a special rain cover that wraps around them. Whether your bag is splash-resistant or not, you may want to take along a few sealable plastic bags for added protection.

A final consideration is moisture condensation. Moving equipment between different environments, for instance from an air-conditioned room to outside, may cause condensation droplets to form in or on the camera. To avoid this, put the equipment into your camera bag until it has had time to adjust to the new temperature.

40 Digital SLR Techniques

Chapter 1

Basic Camera Body Functions

Digital SLR camera bodies provide a wealth of controls allowing you to tailor their performance to your demands. In this chapter, we will discuss possible options for setting up your camera: first, adjustments relating to digital capture, such as ISO and white balance; second, photographic concerns such as metering and focus; and last, a brief section on camera handling.

1

Setting Up the Camera

Most DSLRs have custom functions that allow you to set your preferences as to how the camera works. These settings can be optimized for your normal shooting style, or for a specific project you are undertaking. Properly done, customization can help you get the best photographs more efficiently.

Image Review

▶ ▶ ▶ Instant Review

The default setting for most digital cameras plays back the image on the LCD screen immediately after a photo is taken. This feature gives you instant feedback on what you have captured. Studio or still-life photographers may increase the playback duration to allow for a more thorough check; some cameras allow you to view the image as long as a button is held. Extended use of the LCD screen does drain the battery faster, though.

For sports and portrait photographers, it may be beneficial to switch off instant review. Whether you are trying to shoot the peak of game action or capture that fleeting expression, you probably want to keep your attention on the viewfinder rather than lose an opportunity while glancing at the LCD instead. Images can be reviewed at a more leisurely pace afterward. Also, if image review is not switched off during shooting, your eye may be distracted or irritated by the playback image appearing just below the viewfinder.

▲ Image (left) and image review (right)

▶ ▶ ▶ Histogram Review

You may be able to customize the type of information displayed along with your review image. One useful indicator is the histogram. This is a graph plotting the number of pixels corresponding to each brightness level in the photo. The vertical dimension measures the number of pixels. The horizontal dimension is a distribution of pixel brightness, from total black on the left to total white on the right.

An average scene should have a graph that is more or less evenly spread over the horizontal axis. A higher concentration, or hump, in the middle range would indicate a lot of mid-tone values in the photo.

A histogram with a spike toward the left-hand side could reflect a lot of dark tones, or it could mean that the scene is underexposed. You may then wish to adjust your exposure settings. In this close-up of a lacquer basket, the histogram leans to the left, due to the dark tones of the lacquer.

A histogram with a spike on the right indicates either that the photo is predominantly light, or that it is overexposed.

No matter what, you should take note if the graph goes all the way to the extreme right edge of the histogram: this means that some parts of the image contain no detail whatsoever. Digital editing will not be able to recover any texture there. For the picture of the swans on the following page, the histogram leans to the right, and touches the right edge, indicating that a small region is washed out.

▶ ▶ ▶ Highlight Review

The danger of bleached-out highlights in digital images is such that many cameras offer a highlight review mode. This may be together with or separate from the histogram display. In this review mode, areas of the image with extremely bright values flash to alert you that important detail may be lost. You can see that the bright areas on the swans' heads and necks are the overexposed parts (i.e., touching the right edge of the histogram).

▶ ▶ ▶ Image Rotation

Some cameras have an orientation sensor that can record whether a picture was taken in wide/landscape or tall/portrait orientation. During playback, you may have an option to view the images in the proper orientation. This is good for viewing photos with different orientations without the need to turn the camera itself. However, the screen size of "tall" pictures is much smaller, to fit the wide LCD screen shape. Also, if your camera is already in portrait orientation (e.g., on a tripod), automatic rotation is not needed.

Diopter Correction

Most DSLRs have adjustable diopter correction for those who wish to shoot without wearing their spectacles. Simply adjust the knob or slider till both the viewfinder image and the readout below it are clear. If this is not possible, you may need to use higher diopter attachments which are sold separately.

Image Folders

Certain DSLR models allow you to create and name folders on your memory card, so that the camera will save images according to the folder you choose. This way, you can easily keep pictures from different dates, events, or locations separate for easier organization.

▲ Custom folders

Using Your Camera's Manual

At the beginning, you may need to refer to your camera manual more often to become acquainted with your model's various operations. When you become more experienced, however, you may find just a few pages important for occasional reference. One example is the flash-range table for manual flash output. One suggestion is to take photographs of the desired pages and store them (possibly in a folder of their own) on your memory card. To save space, you may use a smaller image size or lower image quality, as long as the text remains readable on screen. This way, you won't need to carry your manual with you all the time.

▲ Flash range table saved for reference

Firmware Updates

The internal software that controls the DSLR is known as the firmware. Camera manufacturers may offer updates to this firmware to improve performance or fix problems. It is a good idea to check the manufacturer's Web site periodically for available updates. Follow the maker's instructions for installing firmware revisions.

Chapter 1

2

ISO, Image Size, and Quality

Before shooting a sequence, you should be aware of your basic settings for image processing. The ISO setting and image type fundamentally affect the final quality of your pictures, so they should be among the first items on your checklist.

ISO Sensitivity

One of the advantages of digital photography is that the ISO setting may be changed at any time to suit the situation. Stepping from bright sunlight into a dimly lit interior poses no problems, as most DSLRs can be set from ISO 100 or 200 all the way to 800, 1600, or higher.

Note that low ISO settings are better suited to digital sensors. They will capture the finest detail and the smoothest tones, often with no visible noise. This is ideal for landscapes, portraits, and studio photography. Lower ISOs, however, require more light to register on the sensor, so either slower shutter speeds, larger apertures, or brighter lighting are required.

▲ A photo at ISO 200. At this ISO, the photo contains no digital noise.

▲ An enlarged section of the same scene taken at ISO 1600, showing digital noise.

High ISO settings require less light for the sensor; as such, faster shutter speeds, smaller apertures, and dimmer lighting are acceptable. But less light hitting the sensor means that signal levels are low, and DSLRs use signal amplification to increase the sensor output. It is often this processing that results in image noise and lower quality in terms of color and detail. High ISOs, therefore, are more often used for sport and street photography, where flash or slow shutter speeds are not an option.

Thus, you should normally choose the lowest ISO that you estimate to be necessary, and adjust this setting accordingly as the situation changes. Note that ISO is not one of the parameters that can be changed after shooting, even in RAW format; this setting impacts the image at the point of capture.

▶ ▶ ▶ Auto ISO
Some cameras are able to set the ISO automatically, increasing it when the light levels are getting low, and decreasing it when the scene is bright. This can be useful when you are shooting without a tripod, but you should be aware of possible image degradation at high ISOs.

●mage Size

This refers to the number of pixels that make up each image. Depending on your camera, the options may be described by:

● Pixel dimensions, shown as Width × Height

● Total image resolution, given in megapixels

● Descriptive label (e.g., Large, Medium)

For the highest image quality, you should use the largest image size available. This way, you have the option of printing at a larger size, or at a higher output resolution. You'll also be able to crop with greater freedom. You can easily resize your images to make them smaller, while keeping the originals intact.

▲ Image size options, Nikon D70

Use the smaller image sizes only if you are certain that you will never want to crop your images or print at a larger size or resolution. While you can reduce image size easily, you cannot increase it. Your software may provide options for this, but using these will decrease the quality of your photos.

⬤mage Quality

This commonly refers to the choice of file format as well as its compression level, if any.

Two or three JPEG compression levels are available on most cameras. You should select the best quality setting available on your camera model. The best setting uses the least compression, which results in larger files, but retains as much quality as possible. JPEGs can be viewed or edited right out of the camera (without the need for special software), so use this format for a faster workflow with minimal image manipulation.

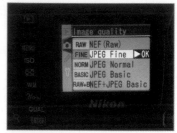

▲ Image quality options, Nikon D70

DSLRs also allow you to shoot in RAW format. You will need the camera manufacturer's own software or a third-party program to convert or edit RAW files. If you have the time to download and process each file on your computer, this may be a good option for you. On the other hand, RAW images can take a prohibitively long time to process if your computer is not powerful enough. They also take up more disk space. If your camera can simultaneously record a RAW file and a good-quality JPEG, this might save you some time, since you can choose to process only those RAW images where the accompanying JPEG is unsatisfactory. Basically, shoot RAW for a workflow that requires careful image manipulation and adjustment of processing parameters.

The TIFF format is available on some DSLRs. This format has the benefits of being lossless, as well as being editable in most programs without having to convert from RAW. There are limitations, though: TIFF files are much larger than RAW files from the same camera, but hold less information. White balance and other parameters are also fixed. The standard DSLR-produced TIFF is only 8-bit, as compared to 12 or 14 for RAW. In the writer's opinion, there is no clear advantage to using this format.

White Balance and Processing Parameters

We will now look at the settings that impact how the information taken from your camera's digital sensor is processed before being stored on your camera as an image file. As these parameters affect the subjective "feel" of a picture, they are important indeed.

White Balance

▶ ▶ ▶ Color Temperature

Whether natural or artificial, different light sources emit different proportions of the various wavelengths of light. Afternoon sunlight turns from golden to blue as the sun goes down. Traditional light bulbs give off an orange light. This color bias is known as color temperature, which is measured in Kelvin (K). A color temperature of 5000-5500K is accepted as standard "daylight" and deemed photographically neutral. A lower color temperature is more orange or red, and a higher one is bluer. See the diagram below for the spectrum of common color temperatures.

3000K	5000K	6000K	8000K
Incandescent	Daylight	Cloudy	Shade

Modern light sources, such as fluorescent and halogen lighting, can have a green or magenta cast (rather than red or blue). The light they emit does not strictly fit in the traditional color temperature model, but they are usually rated according to the part of the traditional scale they are closest to. It is also important to note that some of these lights flicker; though it may not be perceptible to the eye, the color temperature may vary within the time of the camera sensor's exposure. Of additional note is sodium vapor lighting, used in some street lighting; this source emits only orange light (as opposed to a color bias), and thus makes a scene monochromatic.

▶ In this photo, taken at dusk, the indoor and outdoor color temperatures are visibly different.

▶ ▶ ▶ White Balance (WB)

The human brain has the remarkable ability to alter our perception. For example, things that we consider traditionally white might seem white to us even if they are off-white. Other colors can also appear "true" when they are not. One of the wonders of digital photography is its ability to replicate this color compensation, known as white balance (WB). By adjusting the balance between the three RGB channels, a digital camera can make different color temperatures look like "normal" daylight, for instance. Redder light is made bluer (or cooler), while bluer light is made redder (i.e., warmer).

▶ ▶ ▶ WB Presets

Many cameras have presets for the most commonly encountered lighting situations. When you begin photographing in a new location, take some test shots to determine the WB setting you should use.

● **Auto WB (AWB)**: Under good lighting conditions, and especially when there is some white or neutral gray object in the scene, this default setting should produce good results. Auto WB normally has a very wide color temperature range. The better the auto WB, the less you will have to worry about adjusting settings.

- **Incandescent/Tungsten**: Digital cameras often arrange their WB presets in order of increasing color temperature. This setting covers the region around 3000-3500K, and compensates for household filament bulbs and tungsten studio lamps.

▶ Using incandescent WB has corrected the low indoor color temperature, but the evening sky is now unnaturally blue.

- **Fluorescent**: Tube lighting comes in a wide range of colors, such as warm, daylight, and cool; for this reason, it is only an approximation to say that this preset covers the 4200-4500K range. In reality, this setting may cover a wider range, as well as adjust the important green/magenta balance.
- **Sunny/Daylight**: This refers to scenes under direct sunlight, which may be in the 5000-5500K range.
- **Flash**: Electronic flash has a similar color temperature to daylight, but may be slightly cooler (bluer). This setting may be used to good effect when the camera manufacturer's flash units are utilized.
- **Cloudy**: This setting counters the blue cast of the 6000-7000K range, often found indoors without artificial lighting or in the open without direct sunlight.

▶ Auto WB (left) and cloudy WB (right)

● **Shade**: Not found on many compact cameras, this covers the 8000-10000K range, and warms up the color for indoor scenes, those in the shade under very blue skies, or shots from the early morning or evening (without direct sun).

▶ ▶ ▶ Kelvin WB

Some cameras allow you to set the white balance in precise Kelvin units (perhaps to an accuracy of 100K). This could be very accurate, but it could also be difficult if you do not know how to gauge what your eyes see in Kelvin terms, especially for non-traditional artificial lighting. Keep trying out different settings until you become good at gauging scenes in Kelvin units.

▶ ▶ ▶ Custom WB

When automatic or preset WB settings do not give satisfactory results, you can manually set custom white balance. This gives the camera a fixed and precise reference point for processing subsequent images. The main aim is to sample from the lighting that your subject receives, and produce a series of images with consistent white balance.

With some cameras, you need to set the camera to WB measurement mode. Position the camera close to the subject in the same direction as the intended shooting direction. Place a white or neutral gray card (or piece of paper) facing the camera, such that its image fills the entire viewfinder. Make sure that the card is positioned such that the ambient lighting falls on it evenly. Since the card is featureless, switch to manual focus; then release the shutter. The camera measures the white balance and saves the data, but no image is saved to the memory card. This method is quick, but when you set custom WB the next time, you may lose the old setting.

▲ Setting custom WB

Another common method of setting custom WB is to take a photo and save it to your memory card, then set the camera to use that image as a reference for white balance. The procedure is similar to the previous one, except when you release the shutter, the camera takes a picture of your white/gray reference and saves it as an image to your memory card. You then go into the camera menu and select that image as your WB reference. This is slightly more tedious, but is useful when you wish to save WB information.

▲ Selecting the reference image for custom WB

A less frequent application of the previous method is to choose an actual photo of your scene that has suitable WB, and select it as the WB reference. When you are using a WB preset (especially Auto), the camera uses a color temperature range rather than a precise value. You may find that pictures of the same scene have a different color bias, with some photos better white-balanced than others. You can instruct the camera to use the exact WB setting for the best shot obtained with the preset. Using this method does not require a white or gray card, but does depend on your camera's WB preset doing a good job.

An additional method to set custom WB is to use a special diffusing filter (such as an ExpoDisc™) over the lens. This method differs from the other two; the camera (with disc attached) points away from the subject, facing instead in the general direction of the light sources. Outdoors, this might be a generally upward direction; indoors, the lens would have to face midway between the major light sources present. This allows the camera to measure the incident light (the light falling on the subject) directly, rather than the light reflected off a card. If you do not purchase a commercial disc/filter, you can try putting translucent white plastic (such as the cap of a container) or white paper (a flat piece, a cone, or a bleached paper coffee filter) over the lens in the same way. But make sure that you never point the lens at the sun without any diffusion over it. The DSLR mirror is not totally opaque, and the intense light may damage the sensor behind.

▲ Custom WB with paper over lens; the result is slightly too warm.

🎯 Saving Reference Images for Custom WB

No matter what method you use to set custom WB, it is a good idea to save some of your actual photos, shot with custom WB, as reference images. It is easier to identify the location of such WB reference pictures than it is to save indistinguishable pictures of white or gray cards. This can be beneficial if you frequently visit locations with consistent lighting.

If you can create custom folders on your memory card, it can be easy to recall a particular custom WB when you return to the same location and lighting. If you cannot create custom folders, you can protect your WB reference images so that they will not be deleted.

To save space on your memory card, consider taking custom WB photos at a small size or lower quality for reference. You can also select a subject that will clearly indicate where the photo was taken.

▲ Saved WB reference images

▶ ▶ ▶ WB Fine-Tuning and Bracketing

Because of the difficulty in getting a perfect white balance, some cameras allow you to fine-tune WB, either for the presets or for custom WB. The standard adjustment method is to allow control over the traditional red/blue balance. Newer models, such as some Canon DSLRs, allow control over both the blue/amber and magenta/green axes at once.

▲ Four-way WB fine-tuning, Canon EOS 350D/Digital Rebel XT

DSLRs may also have a WB bracketing function. When activated, just one press of the shutter release will suffice; the camera uses one set of sensor data and processes it to produce three pictures: one standard image, one with lower color temperature, and one with higher color temperature. You can choose the degree of bracketing, usually in increments known as "mired." Mired values are calculated by the effect they produce rather than the variation in Kelvin, because the Kelvin scale is not linear. For example, an increase from 3000K to 3100K is equivalent to a shift from 8000K to 8700K.

Green Shift

Blue Shift

Neutral

Amber Shift

Magenta Shift

▲ WB bracketing, Canon EOS 350D/Digital Rebel XT

WB bracketing can be used in conjunction with custom WB. Custom WB may not produce exactly the white balance you want, especially if you use a reference item that is not perfectly neutral. If you are not using a special photographic white or gray reference, this is quite likely. Activate WB bracketing while using custom WB; this will produce images with slightly different white balances. Select the best one, using the menu, as the new custom WB reference. Repeat the process if necessary.

▶ ▶ ▶ Manipulating WB Effects

Some photographs are effective because they have a color cast. Warm candlelight and cool twilight would lose their moods if they were made neutral. You can retain or even create such color casts by choosing WB presets or Kelvin values creatively. Use a lower value, such as the incandescent preset (meant for warmer lighting) to make the scene cooler; use a higher value, such as the shade preset (meant for cooler lighting) to make the scene warmer.

▲ From left: auto, cloudy, and shade WB; the last one captures the warm light of the setting sun.

The same effect can be obtained by using off-white paper to set custom WB. If your surface is blue, your custom WB will be redder; if your surface is green, the resulting cast will be magenta. Think of it as using compensating filters, except that your surface should have the opposite tint of your desired result.

⬤aturation, Contrast, Sharpening, and Hue

DSLRs allow adjustments of other image processing parameters. You can use these settings creatively to achieve a unique look, or in their recommended manners to maximize the potential of your photos.

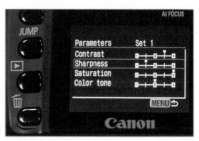

▶ Individual parameter adjustment

▶ ▶ ▶ Parameter Presets

Presets are fixed combinations of processing parameters. The most common presets available are for portraits and nature shots. Portrait presets are usually processed to produce better skin color, reduce the visibility of blemishes and creases, and reduce extreme highlights and shadows. Nature presets usually emphasize vivid colors and sharp detail. Parameter presets may even utilize different color spaces (see the section on color spaces that follows). This is similar to using portrait film or saturated slide film (with a conventional camera) to accentuate certain characteristics in a photo.

▶ ▶ ▶ Saturation

This parameter adjusts color strength. Increase saturation when you want colors to be more bright and vivid; lower the saturation to make colors less strong.

▲ The photo on the left has decreased saturation; on the right, increased saturation.

▶ ▶ ▶ Contrast (Tone)

Contrast refers to the gradation of tones from light to dark. Increase the contrast to make different tones more obvious (e.g., when the scene is too "flat" or dull). Lower the contrast to make tonal gradations smoother (e.g., when there are both bright spots and deep shadows in a scene).

▲ From left: low, normal, and high contrast

Some cameras allow you to upload custom "curves" when the camera is connected to a computer. This lets you control contrast selectively. For example, you could increase mid-tone brightness while maintaining highlight brightness.

▶ ▶ ▶ Sharpening

This is one parameter that should be used with caution. Digital sharpening makes shapes in a photo appear sharper by increasing the contrast along edges and lines. This can be handled by the camera during the shot, or through the use of computer software afterwards. Unsharpened images can look "soft" or unfocused, even if they are in focus. Sharpening effects can correct this, but excessive sharpening can introduce an unnatural appearance to edges and details in the image.

There is no simple formula for the amount of sharpening needed; the output size of the image and the photo's content are two important factors. If you want to edit your photos on your computer, or want to have more options for deciding print size(s), set the camera to apply a lower amount of sharpening. If you want to print your images without further editing, set a higher amount of sharpening. Doing some test prints will help determine the best settings for your camera.

▲ From left: low, normal, and high sharpening

▶ ▶ ▶ Hue (Color Tone)

If you imagine the colors of the rainbow arranged on a wheel, adjusting hue would be like rotating that wheel to shift all the colors by a given amount. In a photo, this effect alters the color spectrum of the entire image. For example, increasing hue shifts the reds in your image toward yellow; decreasing hue shifts the reds toward purple. White, black, and gray, however, are unaffected by hue adjustments.

Hue +9°

Hue Normal

Hue -9°

▲ Hue adjustments: look especially at the orange, yellow, and light blue crayons.

Color Space

The total set of possible colors captured by your camera, and their relationships to each other, are known as a color space. Your DSLR may be able to use two or more color spaces.

▶ ▶ ▶ sRGB

sRGB is the standard color space for most digital cameras, computer monitors, and desktop printers. It is a convenient option for viewing and editing images on a desktop computer.

▶ ▶ ▶ Adobe RGB

This color space has more possible colors than sRGB (i.e., it has a wider gamut). It is suited to more extensive editing and commercial press publication. However, you will need to use appropriate color management and profiles in order to get good results, so use the Adobe RGB space only after you're comfortable with the required workflow.

4

Exposure Modes

We now turn our attention to the photographic operations of a DSLR, which are similar to standard film cameras. Modern SLRs allow you automatic, semi-automatic, and manual control over the exposure. Essentially, these options offer different methods for controlling shutter speed and lens aperture.

Exposure

When you press the shutter release button on the camera, the lens aperture closes to the set value, and the shutter opens for the specified amount of time, exposing the imaging sensor to light coming through the lens. This is what a photographic exposure is. The amount of light needed to form an image on the sensor is determined by the metering system (see Technique 5). To provide this amount of light, you need the correct combination of shutter speed and aperture.

Often, there is more than one possible combination of shutter speed and aperture. One analogy to illustrate this is collecting rainwater in a tin. Assuming that the rain (which corresponds to light) is falling at a constant rate, you could put out a tin with a large mouth (aperture) for a short time (shutter speed), or you could use a tin with a small mouth (aperture) but leave it out for a longer time (shutter speed). Either way, you can collect the same amount of water (exposure).

In photography, light is not measured in linear proportion, but by factors of two. Aperture and shutter speed are both calibrated in steps called "stops." To increase by one stop means to multiply the amount of light by two. To decrease by one stop divides the amount of light by two.

You can exchange stops of aperture for stops of shutter speed. When aperture is enlarged by two stops, for example, shutter speed can be faster by two stops. This maintains the overall exposure.

			Original		
Shutter speed	1/4000s (2 stops faster)	1/2000s (1 stop faster)	1/1000s	1/500s (1 stop slower)	1/250s (2 stops slower)
Aperture	f/2.8 (2 stops larger)	f/4 (1 stop larger)	f/5.6	f/8 (1 stop smaller)	f/11 (2 stops smaller)

▲ A chart showing five combinations of aperture and shutter speed, all resulting in the same exposure.

Program Mode (P)

In this mode, the camera selects both shutter speed and aperture. This is convenient for quick shooting, or passing the camera to someone to take a shot of you. The full range of shutter speeds and apertures is available for the camera to choose from, so you will most likely get an acceptable exposure.

It is common for Program mode to be adjustable. In other words, you can use dials or buttons to choose from other possible shutter-aperture combinations (you don't have to accept the defaults given by your camera). This allows for extra control, somewhat like using the Aperture or Shutter Priority modes.

Aperture Priority Mode (A or Av)

This is a semi-automatic mode. With the lens aperture selected by the user, the camera matches it with a suitable shutter speed. Obviously, the choice of apertures depends on the lens used. Note that the camera may sometimes be unable to provide a matching shutter speed. You will have to change either the aperture or the ISO to stay within the camera's shutter speed range.

One reason to use aperture priority is to control depth of field (DOF). Basically, DOF refers to the part of the scene which appears sufficiently sharp. Shallow DOF means that only a narrow region in the image looks sharp; wide DOF means that a large region in the image—in front of and behind the point of focus—looks sharp.

DOF is dependent on a few factors:

	Aperture	Focal Length	Focus Distance	Viewing Size
Less DOF	Larger	Longer	Closer	Larger
More DOF	Smaller	Shorter	Farther	Smaller

To obtain shallow DOF, you should use a large aperture (e.g., f/2.8), a lens with a long focal length (e.g., 135mm), and get close to your subject (e.g., 2m). This is often done when you wish to isolate your subject from the foreground and background. The subject will stand out more clearly.

▲ f/2.8, 1/3200s   ▲ f/5.6, 1/1000s   ▲ f/11, 1/250s

To get maximum DOF, you should use a small aperture (e.g., f/16), a short focal length (e.g., 24mm), and stand farther from your subject (e.g., 20m). This is often done in landscape and architectural photography, when you want to capture the detail in the entire scene.

See the sample photos above. DOF increases as the aperture decreases (from left to right). Detail on the two lions in the background is more visible, but so are background distractions. (Note: the shutter speed for the photo at left is not the expected 1/4000s due to changing sunlight brightness.)

DOF is also affected by viewing size. The same picture, when viewed under different conditions, can have different apparent DOF. When viewing a 4" × 6" print at arm's length, most objects will seem sharp, but peering closely at a 12" × 18" print will probably reveal that less of the scene is acceptably sharp at that magnification.

A second reason to use aperture priority is to control the shutter speed. A larger aperture lets in more light, so a faster shutter speed may be used. Therefore, to make sure the camera uses the fastest matching shutter speed, set the aperture to a large (or the largest) setting. This is useful when shooting action or in dim light. Conversely, set a small aperture to ensure the camera sets a slower shutter speed. This is useful when you want to capture motion as streaks (e.g., a waterfall, or vehicle headlights).

Shutter Priority Mode (S or Tv)

Similar to aperture priority, this is a semi-automatic mode, except that the shutter speed is set by the user, and the camera attempts to provide a matching aperture. If no suitable aperture is available, you will have to change the shutter speed or the ISO.

Set a higher shutter speed when you want to minimize image blur caused by movement. Either the subject could be moving, or you might be shooting from a moving vehicle. The shutter speed needed depends on the speed and direction of movement. For example, motion directly towards or away from you is not as significant as motion from left to right. Also, motion close to you is more obvious than the same amount of motion far away.

Because fast shutter speeds expose the sensor for only a short period of time, either a larger aperture or higher ISO may be needed. If using flash, you will also have to stay within the camera's maximum flash-sync speed.

Use slower shutter speeds to show motion blur. This can portray motion more effectively than freezing it with a fast shutter speed. If you keep still, the moving subject will be blurred. If you follow the subject by panning the camera along in the same direction of movement, the background will be blurred instead.

▶ Panning leaves only the head and torso distinct.

Slower shutter speeds are also useful when using flash. In dim environments, flash with a higher shutter speed (e.g., 1/125s) may light the subject well but leave the background too dark to be seen. Using flash with a slower shutter speed (e.g. 1/30s)—sometimes called "dragging" the shutter—will allow the background to appear more visibly.

Manual Mode (M)

In Manual mode, the shutter speed and aperture settings are left to you to control. Usually, the camera will provide a graphical or numerical display to show you the difference between your exposure setting and the suggested amount. A plus symbol indicates that you are giving greater exposure than suggested; a minus symbol indicates less exposure.

This mode is useful when photographing subjects that could fool the camera's exposure meter. White subjects, such as snow and wedding dresses, may make the camera think that the lighting is brighter than it is; dark subjects, such as deep shadows or black tuxedos, may give the impression of dimness. You can set manual exposure based on other parts of the scene, and then continue photographing without worrying about variations in the brightness of your subjects. This will work as long as the light level remains the same.

You would also use Manual mode when using an external light meter, or when controlling the light level by varying flash output. In these cases the camera's settings will be determined solely by your calculations.

Preset Modes

DSLRs that are marketed at novices or beginners may have preset exposure modes alongside those above. These may include a fully auto or "green" mode, as well as presets for common subjects such as portraits, landscapes, sport, and night scenes. These preset modes are not really necessary; you can control aperture to give less or more DOF for portraits and landscapes respectively, and you can select fast and slow shutter speeds for sport and night scenes, respectively.

These modes usually limit your control of camera functions. The flash may fire automatically, and the camera may take control of WB and ISO. In addition, you may have no choice over parameters such as contrast and sharpening. Because of all these limitations, use preset or scene modes with caution.

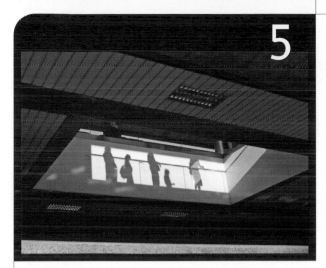

5

Metering Modes

In the previous section, we learned that the camera can suggest suitable shutter speeds and apertures to get a good exposure. We will now explore metering, which is how the camera calculates exposure.

"Correct" Exposure

The first consideration in calculating exposure is the ISO setting of the sensor. Lower ISOs have less sensitivity and therefore require that a greater amount of light reaches the sensor. Higher ISOs are more sensitive and need less light. ISO ratings are, as may be expected, calibrated in stops. Common ratings are 100, 200, 400, and 800–each one stop higher than the previous one.

This still begs the question of what effect the light is supposed to have on the sensor. Basically, it is supposed to accurately record an "average" scene? The assumption is that most of the pixels in an average scene will fall halfway between black and white (i.e., they will be mid-tones of whatever colors populate the scene). Of course, this is not always true.

The photograph of white paper on the following page illustrates the point. Since no camera can actually know what it is pointed at, the result is a completely gray image–not white. The histogram shows a spike squarely in the center representing all the gray pixels. Understandably, this was not a fair test as there is only one tone in this scene.

Modern cameras are able to expose for normal photographic scenes containing bright, medium, and dark areas. They do this using one or more metering patterns to calculate a suitable exposure for a scene.

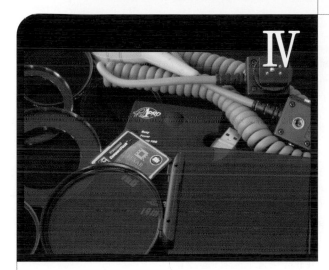

Accessorizing

The DSLR photographer is presented with a mind-boggling assortment of add-ons for the basic camera body. This section outlines some of the options available.

Lenses

It used to be said that the camera body didn't matter so long as you used pro film and pro lenses. With DSLRs, that may not be true, as you commit yourself to one combination of sensor and processing. Still, it is true that the sensor can only capture what the lens gives it. A better lens gives the capability to capture a better image.

▶ ▶ ▶ Focal Length

A lens is primarily identified by its focal length, which determines how much of the scene is captured. A shorter focal length (e.g., 18mm) takes in a wider view, while a longer one (e.g., 200mm) takes in a narrower view.

▲ Scene taken at 18mm focal length   ▲ Part of the same scene at 200mm

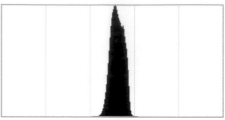

Multi-Segment Metering

These metering patterns subdivide the image area into numerous segments. The camera is programmed to compare the overall brightness within each segment before calculating the exposure. This way, the camera is less likely to be fooled by unusual areas of brightness in some segments—such as the sun or patches of snow.

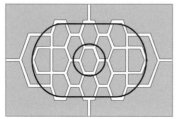
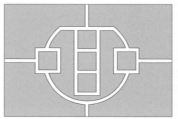

▲ From left: Canon evaluative metering; Nikon matrix metering; this high-contrast scene might benefit from multi-segment metering.

Center-Weighted Metering

This is a classic metering pattern. Some of the old film cameras have it as their only metering pattern. It has two basic areas: the center circle and the rest of the frame. More weight is given to the brightness within the circle—typically 60-75%. The rest is given to the outer frame. This pattern is suited for pictures where the subject is in the center. It is more susceptible to errors in scenes where no average mid-tone subject exists.

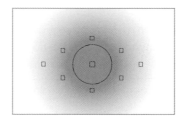

▶ Center-weighted metering and a typical subject for which it is well-suited.

Spot and Partial Metering

These patterns are useful in situations where much of the scene is either very dark or very bright, or where you need to sample the light level from just one part of the scene. The area for partial metering is small, and even smaller for spot metering. In the images below, only the highlighted areas are used to calculate exposure; the rest of the frame is ignored.

 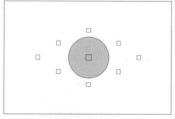

◀ Spot (left) and partial (right) metering patterns

◀ Left. Multi-segment metering is slightly underexposed.
Right: Spot metering the lampshade gives a better result.

Fine-Tuning Exposure

Sometimes, looking at the scene or reviewing the image histogram will indicate that the camera will have problems calculating exposure without your help. In scenes where there are bright lights (e.g., the sun) or where lighter tones predominate (e.g., a snow-covered landscape), the camera may interpret them as mid-tones. The resulting picture will be underexposed, darker than it should be. In scenes with predominantly dark tones or shadows (e.g., some night scenes), the camera may render these as mid-tones. The photo will be overexposed.

There are a few ways to arrive at the correct exposure for your photo, so that whites and blacks will be correctly rendered in the final image.

▶ ▶ ▶ Exposure Compensation

You can dial in exposure compensation in half or third stops. Compensating to the + side increases the overall exposure, making the image brighter. Light colors may require +0.5 stop. White areas may need +1 to +1.5 stops. Compensating to the - side decreases exposure, so the picture will become darker. Try up to -1 stop for very dark areas.

▲ White paper: +1.7 stops exposure

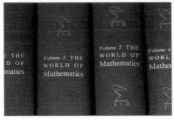

▲ Dark green books: -0.7 stops exposure

▶ ▶ ▶ Auto Exposure Bracketing

DSLRs have a range of exposure bracketing options. Bracketing means taking a series of photos, one with the camera's suggested exposure, and the rest brighter or darker by the amount of bracketing you set. Unlike WB bracketing, you will need to release the shutter once for each variation, since the camera requires a different exposure level each time. The camera will vary the shutter speed, aperture, or ISO, depending on the exposure mode and camera model. You can review the results and delete the unsatisfactory exposures.

▶ ▶ ▶ Meter Only the Mid-tones

If you can isolate the mid-tones, your camera will be able to give the correct exposure. If you have spot or partial metering, place the small metering circle over an area in the scene that has mid-tones. Lock the exposure that is given, compose your picture, and release the shutter.

If you don't have spot or partial metering, you may be able to obtain a mid-tone reading by going close to a mid-tone area within the scene so that the camera can meter from it. This is not always possible, especially if that area is far away. Another option is to meter from a mid-tone area outside the scene, but in the same light as your final scene. Again, after using the mid-tones to get a correct exposure reading, lock the exposure before shifting the camera back to the original view. Refer to your camera manual for instruction on using exposure lock.

Tonal Range

So far we have been dealing with the correct exposure for parts of the image that are mid-toned. In an ideal scene, when the mid-tones are properly exposed, the bright and dark regions will fall into place accordingly. In reality, the sensor can only capture a fixed range of brightness levels. This is its tonal range. Sometimes, the scene contains extremely dark and extremely bright areas, such that the tonal range of the scene exceeds the camera's. Apart from using flash or filters to adjust the tonal range, you will have to choose between the following:

- **Expose for the highlights(below, left)**: This means setting exposure so that the bright areas do not hit the right end of the histogram and become overexposed. The rest of the image, however, will fall to the left end of the histogram, and may appear underexposed. Many feel that underexposure is better than overexposure, because you can recover shadow detail by editing the image on a computer. This is true, but recovered detail may not be of the best quality.

- **Expose for the mid-tones(below, center)**: This choice concentrates on making the mid-tones appear correct. The brightest and darkest regions, however, may turn to total white and black, respectively. This may be done when only the mid-tone areas are important.

- **Expose for the shadows(below, right)**: This attempts to prevent the dark regions of the picture from hitting the left of the histogram and becoming underexposed. This is traditionally done with negative film, but is not recommended for digital capture as the brighter regions will be irreversibly washed out.

▲ Metering the white pot retains detail in the ceramic surface, but the rest of the image is underexposed.

▲ Metering the mid-toned green of the leaves gives a balanced exposure, but the pot is overexposed.

▲ Metering the dark ironwork causes a loss of detail in the brighter regions.

Chapter 1

6 Focusing

This section will give a short overview of the common focusing modes. You may choose to rely on the wonders of modern autofocus (AF) technology, or take control with manual focus.

Single-Shot AF

When the distance between you and your subject is fixed, this is the normal setting used. Point your camera so that its AF sensor hits your subject. A light press of the shutter button activates AF. When focus is confirmed, the camera gives a signal in the viewfinder and focusing stops. The focus will be locked at the current position as long as you keep the button half-pressed. You can now frame your picture (even if the AF sensor no longer touches the subject) before pressing the shutter button down fully to take a picture. Usually, the camera will not fire if correct focus is not obtained. This is known as focus-priority.

Continuous AF

This is used mostly for sport or action photography, when the subject (or photographer) is continuously moving. With an AF sensor on the subject, press the shutter button halfway. The camera will continuously focus as long as the button is half-pressed. When the button is fully pressed, the camera will take a picture no matter whether the image was in perfect focus or not. This is called release-priority.

▶ Continuous AF has kept this fast-moving skater in focus.

Manual Focus (MF)

Autofocus may not operate well in some conditions, such as when the scene is too dim, when the subject lacks areas of clear contrast, when shooting through a cage, or when the subject is moving too fast or erratically. In these situations, manual focus may give better results.

Switch to manual focus (via the camera body or the lens) before turning the focus ring by hand. Lenses using ultrasonic motors may be manually focused while in AF mode, but standard autofocus lenses should only be focused manually in MF mode, otherwise the AF motor may be damaged.

▲ AF/MF switches on both lens and camera body

Focus until the subject appears the sharpest in the viewfinder. The subject can be anywhere in the frame, so it is possible to compose the picture before focusing. But if you focus manually with an AF sensor on your subject, the camera will usually show a focus confirmation signal when you have reached the point of sharp focus. This feedback can be useful when precise focus is hard to gauge visually.

Manual focus can also be used when you want to maximize DOF using a small aperture. With a wide-angle lens, set the focus about one-third of the distance from your camera into the region that you want the DOF to cover. For example, if you want the scene from 5m to 50m to be sharp, the total depth is 45m. You would therefore focus approximately 15m into the scene, or at 20m distance from your camera. With a telephoto lens, you should focus halfway into the DOF region. These ratios are only approximate; you should use the DOF preview button on your camera, if there is one, to check whether the DOF actually covers the intended range. You can also review the image on the LCD in place of DOF preview.

Multiple AF Sensors

Most DSLRs have more than one AF sensor, and you will have the choice of using one or more at the same time. Activate all of them if your subject is quite obvious and is the closest object in the frame, especially if it is moving around. The combination of sensors will be able to cover more of the frame and allow you to acquire focus more quickly.

Use only the central sensor if your subject is not conspicuous, or if there are other objects in the viewfinder which are closer. Using one AF point removes interference from the other AF sensors, which may focus on other objects. Additionally, the central AF point usually has high sensitivity; the others might be less sensitive. It should be chosen when the situation is more demanding, such as during fast action.

You may use one of the outer AF sensors instead of the central one if you wish to place the subject off-center in the frame. This might be faster than locking focus with the central sensor before composing the picture.

A-DEP Mode

This mode is found on some Canon DSLRs. It is actually a combination of exposure and focus modes. Standing for Automatic Depth (of field), A-DEP uses all of the camera's AF sensors to detect the nearest and farthest points covered by them. Then, it selects an aperture that will provide enough DOF to cover that range. Finally, it sets focus such that the resulting DOF will extend over the selected scene.

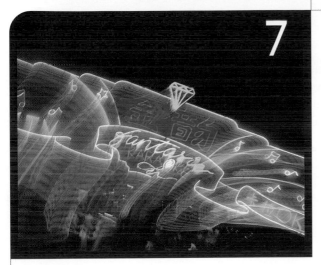

7

Camera Handling

We will end this chapter with a brief mention of some techniques for holding the camera steady. While a tripod will certainly minimize camera shake, and should be used where possible, it is not always expedient to use one.

Stability

Position yourself such that you will be able to frame your picture comfortably. If you have no choice but to assume an off-balance position for some time, take a break every now and then, or you might begin to shake from the effort. Avoid unnecessary muscle tension, such as hunching your shoulders or raising your elbows away from your body. Stay aware of what your body is doing, especially if there is a lot of excitement going on around you.

Use other support for your camera or arms where available (e.g., your bag or a tabletop). When resting your arms on something, it is better to support your forearms rather than the points of your elbows. If you are not on stable ground, however–in a rattling bus, for example–it will probably be better to stay away from vibrating surfaces and let your body act as a shock absorber. You may even bend your knees to counter any jolts.

▶ The standard position for landscape-format photos, with arms close to the body (left). For portrait-format photos, the left arm is tucked in to support the camera and lens (right).

Grip

DSLRs are large and heavy compared to compact cameras, but they are designed to give your right hand a comfortable grip, while your left hand cradles the lens and camera base. In most situations, there is no need to fear that the camera will fall out of your hands, so don't exert a lot of force when holding the camera. Handle it with a light touch and just let its weight fall into your cupped hands.

Press the shutter release gently until the picture is taken; do not stab at the button. Using the flat part of the forefinger near the first finger joint may give you better control than the tip near the fingernail.

▶ Putting the flat of the finger on the shutter release

Breathing

Your heartbeat and breathing cause minor camera movement. Of course, the former must continue, but take some time to calm down if your heart is pumping faster than normal. Breathing, however, can be put on hold for a few seconds while you take the picture. When ready to take the photo, either breathe in or out slightly, hold your breath, and press the shutter button slowly. Make sure you keep still until the mirror noise is over and the viewfinder has cleared. Don't move off too soon. If the attempt was unsuccessful, recover your breathing until the next opportunity for a shot arises.

40 Digital SLR Techniques

Extendable Features and Techniques

We turn our attention now to the use of lenses and flash. Each DSLR system is compatible with dozens of lenses, enabling you to express your creative vision. The use of flash can enhance your camera's performance by adding to or modifying the light on your subject.

8

Lenses & Sensor Size

Due to the fact that DSLRs may have sensors of differing sizes, using the same lens focal length may give you quite different results with different models. If you are bringing over existing lenses from your film SLR system, you may find the "new look" rather unusual. If your digital camera is your first foray into the SLR world, though, there is little to adjust to.

35mm Equivalent

Many people have used 35mm film cameras for the last few decades, and it has been a stable format: almost all 35mm cameras—with the exception of a few half-frame and panoramic models—produce images measuring 36mm × 24mm. As a result of this history, it's easy to compare other cameras, such as DSLRs, to the established 35mm system.

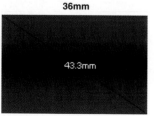

◀ The 35mm film frame has a diagonal of 43.3mm. This is the standard to which the various DSLR sensors are compared.

Field-of-View (FOV) Crop

Most DSLRs have a sensor smaller than a 35mm film frame. Thus, their field-of-view (FOV) is smaller than that of a 35mm film SLR. The ratio of the diagonal of 35mm film (43.3mm) to the sensor's diagonal is called the FOV crop.

36mm

◄ Some DSLRs, such as the Canon EOS 1Ds and Kodak DSLR/n, have sensors the same size as a 35mm film frame. They are thus called full-frame DSLRs. These DSLRs will give the same FOV as a 35mm film camera.

36mm

◄ The Canon EOS 1D Mk II has a sensor diagonal of about 34.5mm; therefore it has an FOV crop of about 1.3.

36mm

◄ Quite a few models, including Nikon DSLRs, have an FOV crop of about 1.5. Some Canon DSLRs have an FOV crop of roughly 1.6. Sigma DSLRs, using Foveon sensors, have an FOV crop of around 1.7.

36mm

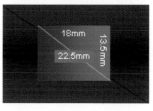

◄ Olympus E-series DSLRs have 4/3-size sensors with an approximate FOV crop of 2. In addition, the sensor proportions are 4:3 instead of 35mm film's 3:2.

Focal Length "Multiplier" Effect

Because of the FOV crop, the view through the same lens looks narrower on most DSLRs as compared to a 35mm SLR. The FOV crop is also described as a focal length multiplier (FLM). When you use a lens of a given focal length on a DSLR, it seems as if you are using a 35mm lens of that focal length multiplied by the FOV crop factor. So, if you use a 35mm lens on a DSLR with an FOV crop of 1.5, the view will look like that of a 50mm lens on a 35mm SLR.

▲ Views through a 35mm lens: SLR (red frame)   ▲ View through a 50mm lens on a 35mm SLR
   and DSLR with 1.5 FOV crop (yellow frame)

Sports and nature photographers may find the cropped DSLR view to their advantage. A 300mm lens can now seem like a 450mm lens, assuming a 1.5 FOV crop. The apparent gain in focal length makes it easier to fill the frame with the selected athlete or wildlife.

For landscape and wide-angle enthusiasts, the multiplication of focal length will probably not be a good thing. With an FOV crop of 1.6, a wide 20mm lens will now give pictures that look as if they were taken with a 32mm lens. With a smaller sensor, it becomes harder to capture the sweeping expanse in front of you.

Photographers with a collection of lenses will find that they have to calculate the new equivalent focal lengths their lenses take on with the move to digital. They may find that their old lenses are no longer as suitable for their work. Fortunately for newcomers, a fresh start makes it easier to get the right range of focal lengths.

Magnification

No matter what FOV crop there is, using the same lens will render the subject the same size. A smaller sensor merely captures the central portion of what the lens projects, and there is no change in the lens' magnifying power. However, an FOV crop may give the impression that the scene is magnified. This is because the digital image has to be enlarged to fill the same space as a 35mm image. This is no different than enlarging just the central portion of the 35mm frame.

Depth of Field

Because DOF is dependent on the actual focal length of a lens, rather than the apparent one, do not use the multiplied focal length to calculate DOF. Instead, use the actual focal length of the lens to gauge DOF. A 50mm lens always gives the same DOF, whether the DSLR sensor has an FOV crop or not. The focal length may seem to multiply, but the DOF does not.

Nevertheless, the FOV crop may affect the apparent DOF of a print, simply because DOF is also affected by viewing size. An image from a smaller sensor may need greater enlargement, compared to a larger sensor, when printed to a fixed size. Greater enlargement tends to reduce the apparent DOF.

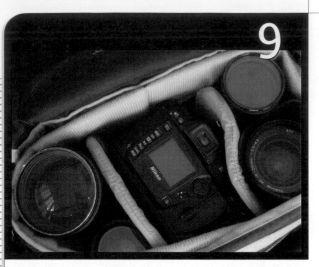

9

Types of Lenses

While DSLR lenses may not have the convenience or compactness of the 10× or 12× zoom lenses that some compact cameras offer, they make up for it by their sheer range. Combined with a DSLR body, many of these lenses are capable of image quality unmatched by compact or prosumer cameras.

Lens Specifications

While lenses may be mainly characterized by their focal lengths, there are other factors affecting their performance.

▶ ▶ ▶ Maximum and Minimum Apertures

Aperture is the ratio of lens diameter to its focal length. Large-aperture lenses require more material and are more difficult to design, and are therefore more expensive. These factors are amplified with long focal lengths. Thus, while a 50mm, f/1.8 lens is relatively cheap, a 600mm, f/4 lens has an enormous size and price.

Large apertures are often worth the cost if you need faster shutter speeds in low-light situations, or if you wish to minimize DOF. At maximum aperture, however, lenses may suffer from aberrations that degrade image quality. See the image to the right for an example of this effect.

▶ Note the color "blooming" around each flower petal at f/2.8.

Small apertures allow you to maximize DOF. At very small apertures, however, an effect known as diffraction will affect the overall image sharpness. Depending on the exact equipment used, you may wish to be cautious with apertures smaller than f/11. Use them only when you must give up some sharpness in order to gain DOF.

▶ Left: Close-up of petal at f/8; not much DOF
▶▶ Right: Close-up of petal at f/32; improved DOF, but a slight loss of sharpness

▶▶▶ Maximum Magnification

A magnification of 1:4 means that the image of the subject on the sensor is a quarter of its actual size. Maximum magnification refers to the largest size ratio a lense can achieve. Lenses with greater maximum the magnifications (such as 1:4) are sometimes said to have "macro" capability. Technically, this refers to lenses made to give 1:1 (i.e., life-size) magnification or larger, but the term is used rather loosely to mean greater magnification than "normal."

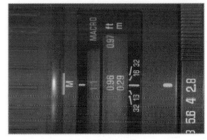

▲ The Tamron 90mm macro lens has true 1:1 capability.

▶▶▶ Minimum Focus Distance

The closer you get to your subject, the larger it will be on the sensor. Macro lenses are designed to focus closer than normal lenses, thus producing greater magnification. Macro photographers are also interested in the minimum focus distance because it affects the working distance; this is the distance from the front of the lens to the subject. Two lenses may give 1:1 magnification, but the one with the longer working distance will be preferred for shy or flighty macro subjects. This way, you can achieve high magnification without getting too close to your subject.

▶ ▶ ▶ Special Lens Materials and Design

Specially formulated materials, such as low-dispersion glass, are used in some lenses. In addition, some lens elements are aspherical or use diffractive optics for improved optical performance or reduction in bulk. As a photographer, you should read reviews by actual users of lenses to gauge how they perform, rather than focus too much on lens construction.

There are some design aspects that are highly relevant to practical photography. The first is whether the front element (the foremost end of the lens) rotates when the lens is focused. If it does, attached graduated and polarizing filters will also rotate. This makes work more cumbersome. The second aspect is internal or rear focusing. Typically, lens barrels extend—sometimes significantly—when focused at closer distances. Lenses with internal or rear focusing move the smaller inner lens elements instead, resulting in less physical movement of lens parts. This is beneficial, as AF can be quieter and faster. The lens size also remains more or less constant.

▲ The AF-S Nikkor 18-70 on the left and the Tamron 90mm SP on the right, both focused at infinity.

▲ When focused at around 0.38m, the internal-focusing Nikkor remains the same size.

▶ ▶ ▶ Ultrasonic AF

Earlier autofocus technology used small motors placed in either the lens or camera body to move the lens elements. The newest AF technology employs ultrasonic motors, which are faster and nearly silent in operation. The best type of ultrasonic AF design (e.g., Canon's ring-type USM) keeps the autofocus separate from the manual focus ring. You can take over and focus manually without switching to MF mode. This is good for making quick focus adjustments.

▲ The M/A switch on this AF-S (ultrasonic) lens allows immediate MF override.

Overall, lenses using ultrasonic motors are desirable if you need fast or discreet AF. If your interests are more in landscape or still life, this technology is unnecessary.

▶ ▶ ▶ Image Stabilization

When the camera and lens are handheld, minor movement causes the image projected on the sensor to be shaky. As a result, pictures may be blurred. Image stabilization lenses counter this movement using internal lens elements. These elements attempt to keep the image in the same place on the sensor, thus ensuring a sharper image.

Depending on your equipment setup and handling technique, using image stabilizing lenses can help you get sharp pictures with shutter speeds up to two or three stops slower than normal.

When the camera is secured on a tripod, you may need to turn off the stabilization. Otherwise, some lenses may over-compensate their stabilizing attempts, resulting (ironically) in some image blur.

For camera panning, some lenses have an option to stabilize only vertical vibration, so that your panning will be captured correctly. For some older lenses without this option, stabilization may again have to be switched off. Otherwise, the system will attempt to negate your panning motion.

Newer image stabilizing lenses have the ability to modify their action such that they will not interfere with tripod use and panning. You may leave stabilization on if it improves your images, or switch it off to conserve battery power.

▶ ▶ ▶ Distortion

This refers to the way that straight lines are recorded as curves in a photo, especially near the edges of the picture.

 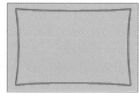

- ▶ Left: Barrel distortion makes lines curve outward at the center of the frame edges, thus taking on a barrel shape.
- ▶ ▶ Right: Pincushion distortion makes lines curve inward at the centers of the frame edges, taking on a slightly star-like shape.

Some lenses have irregular distortion, producing lines that are wavy like a gentle W shape.

For architecture and flat copying, it is important to have as little distortion as possible. Computer software may be used to correct distortion, but this will also take additional time. Barrel and pincushion distortion are relatively easy to correct, but irregular distortion can be tricky to straighten out.

Many lenses exhibit mild distortion, and zoom lenses may even change from one type of distortion to another as you zoom. For subjects without straight lines (such as many outdoor scenes), distortion may not affect the photo drastically. For some photographers, distortion can be used creatively. Eventually, you must decide whether the distortion produced by a lens is acceptable for your photos.

▶ ▶ ▶ Vignetting

This refers to uneven illumination across the image, especially at a lens' maximum aperture. The corners of the picture are often darker than the center, and this is called vignetting or light falloff. The amount is measured in stops: a half-stop falloff means that the corners look as if they received half a stop less exposure.

Vignetting normally decreases when a lens is stopped down (i.e., an aperture smaller than maximum is used). If you can stop down to f/5.6 or f/8, vignetting will not be a problem most of the time. For portrait and candid photography, however, maximum aperture may be used frequently. If you are purchasing large-aperture lenses, you should be aware of the amount of vignetting, though it might not always be unpleasant.

An easy way to check for vignetting is to switch the camera to aperture-priority mode and set the lens at maximum aperture. Take a photo of an evenly lit plain surface, such as white paper, using manual focus. Make sure the illumination is even, and that no shadows are intruding. Reviewing the image on the LCD or computer should show you the amount of vignetting.

▲ Slight vignetting can be seen in the corners.

▶ ▶ ▶ Bokeh

Said to be derived from Japanese, this term refers to the way a lens renders the out-of-focus regions in a photo. When not in focus, a point of light is seen as a circle. The nature of the out-of-focus points and the way they combine all affect the overall look of the blurred regions of a picture (often the background).

▲ Bokeh from the AF Nikkor 80-200mm f/2.8 (early version)

▲ Bokeh from the Sigma 70-300mm DL Macro

▲ Bokeh from the Tamron 90mm SP Macro

▲ Mirror lenses give doughnut-like out-of-focus circles, which are generally considered bad bokeh

Bokeh is important for some portraiture and nature photography, where a large aperture is used to blur the background and make the subject stand out. However, it is also a subjective characteristic that cannot be quantified. You should look at test shots—at varying apertures, possibly—to see for yourself.

▶ ▶ ▶ Lens Sharpness and Contrast

The ability of lenses to resolve fine detail commands a great deal of attention from product reviewers. Doing controlled tests, reviewers produce MTF (modulation transfer function) curves on a scale of 100, which basically show how successfully a lens resolves precisely spaced pairs of black and white lines (measured in line pairs per mm, or lp/mm). Good MTF values at 10 lp/mm indicate that a lens produces high contrast, while good MTF values at 40 lp/mm indicate that it can render fine detail such as eyelashes.

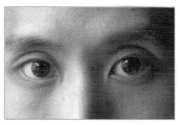

▲ Sharp rendering of eyebrows and lashes

Before becoming obsessed with MTF charts, however, you should note that most lenses produce their best sharpness and contrast when stopped down between f/5.6 and f/11 (depending on the lens). They also tend to perform better when not at their minimum focusing distance, and (for zooms) not at the extreme focal lengths. You should evaluate your own needs and run your own tests, since most current lenses can produce excellent results when used at their optimum settings.

Overall, the quality of a lens is a relatively subjective judgement, depending on your priorities and needs. Consider the characteristics above—as well as the price—when making your decisions.

▶ ▶ ▶ Digital-Only Lenses

Digital sensors produce the best images when the light rays from the lens strike the sensor straight on, rather than at an angle. Lenses designed for film may not allow this, because film does not suffer the same limitations.

Legacy lenses were also designed so that they project an image circle onto the 35mm film frame, large enough to cover it without too much vignetting. Digital sensors are smaller, and thus the outer region of 35mm lenses' image circles is wasted. You do, however, use the best part of the lens, its center.

Digital-only lenses are designed to address both issues. Their lens elements direct the light rays in a more parallel path onto the sensor. They are also smaller and lighter than their 35mm counterparts because they produce smaller image circles covering sensors with FOV crops of 1.5 or more.

As a result, these lenses cannot be used on film SLRs, or full-frame and 1.3 FOV crop DSLRs, because the edges of the picture would have no image projected onto them. Canon's newer EF-S lenses should not even be mounted on incompatible cameras, as releasing the shutter may damage the camera and lens.

Prime Lenses

These are lenses with fixed focal lengths. Generally easier to design, they often have larger apertures, better sharpness, and lower distortion than zooms. The trade-off is that you may have to carry a bag full of lenses to cover different situations; changing lenses will also take up time, and increase the possibility of dust entering the lens mount.

▶ ▶ ▶ Extreme Wide-Angle and Fisheye

These are around 14mm or 16mm for the full 35mm frame format. For smaller sensors, this would be around 10.5mm. These lenses capture virtually everything in front of the camera, giving very dramatic views or enabling wide shots in enclosed spaces. Image distortion can be quite high, with nearby objects appearing huge, and lines appearing strongly curved.

▶ ▶ ▶ Wide-Angle

For 35mm, this would include the 17mm to 35mm range; for smaller sensors, around 10mm to 24mm. These lenses take in a wide expanse of scenery. They exaggerate perspective and the distance between objects.

▲ A wide-angle view frames the clouds over the houses.

▲ A wide-angle lens distorts proportions when used up close.

▶ ▶ ▶ Normal

Normal lenses are defined as having focal lengths about the same as the film or sensor diagonal. For 35mm cameras, the diagonal is around 43mm, so any lens from 40mm to 58mm could be called a "normal" lens. For smaller sensors, the sensor diagonal could be somewhere between 23mm and 35mm. Normal lenses are often said to portray objects with natural perspective, but this does depend on the size of your prints.

▲ A simple shot of newlyweds

Quite a few manufacturers also offer normal focal length macro lenses for the 35mm format. Some of them require the use of a special adapter to reach 1:1 magnification.

▲ A normal focal length is acceptable for a half-body shot.

▶ ▶ ▶ Short Telephoto

Comprising the 80mm to 135mm range in the 35mm format, this group is commonly used for portraits because of the limited DOF that isolates the subject from its surroundings. These focal lengths also allow the photographer to get a chest-up portrait at a comfortable distance from the subject. For smaller sensors, the corresponding range would be about 50mm to 90mm.

▲ A short telephoto focal length gives a more natural perspective with similar framing.

▲ You can get in close and frame your subject tightly.

Macro lens designs in the short telephoto range are quite popular. Ranging from 90mm to 105mm, they usually focus at 1:1 magnification without any further accessories.

▶ ▶ ▶ Long Telephoto

This group is generally 180mm and up in 35mm; in smaller-format digital, the range begins in the region of 100mm to 135mm and goes up from there. Telephoto lenses compress the sense of perspective and make objects at different distances look "stacked" together. Often used for sport and nature photography, this group of lenses has applications in many areas. They allow you to get a very close view from afar.

Note: Perspective depends on the distance to the subject, not the lens used. However, photographers often adjust their shooting distance in order to achieve a certain framing.

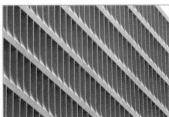

▲ A long telephoto turns the building facade into an abstract pattern.

◀ Too long a focal length can flatten features too much.

▶ ▶ ▶ Special Lens Designs

● **Mirror lenses** are compact and light compared to standard lenses of equal focal length. This is because they are constructed using mirrors instead of heavier glass elements. The main disadvantage is that the aperture of a mirror lens is fixed, and usually not very large. Some people also dislike the typical mirror lens bokeh.

▲ The construction of a mirror lens explains its doughnut-like bokeh.

● **Perspective-control lenses**, also known as tilt/shift lenses, let you shift the lens elements parallel to the sensor plane or tilt them away from the lens' central axis—while the lens is attached. This allows you to correct perspective problems, such as converging vertical lines caused by pointing the camera upward or downward. They are quite costly, being made for specialized purposes. If you do not need tilt/shift control frequently, perspective can also be changed using software such as Photoshop.

▲ A standard perspective-control lens

Zoom Lenses

If your DSLR was bundled with a kit lens, you probably have a zoom lens. Zoom lenses allow you to vary the focal length with a twist of the zoom ring, giving you the equivalent of many lenses in one, and allowing you to fine-tune your framing without moving the camera. In the past, zoom lenses produced inferior pictures compared to prime lenses, but modern designs have improved to the extent that the best zooms outperform some primes.

Cheaper zoom lenses have variable maximum apertures. At wider angles, the maximum aperture is larger; as you zoom to a longer focal length, this maximum aperture decreases. Coupled with the fact that longer focal lengths are more difficult to hold steady, this makes the wider end of the zoom range more suitable for low-light photography.

Some zoom lenses have constant maximum apertures. They are necessarily bigger and heavier than the variable-aperture zooms, but most of them are made to high standards for professional use, and give very good performance. The best ones are equal to a set of prime lenses.

▶ ▶ ▶ Wide-Angle Zooms

These normally have a 2x range, commonly 17-35mm for 35mm format. The photojournalist's popular constant-aperture 17-35mm is equivalent to 17mm, 20mm, 24mm, 28mm, and 35mm lenses—all with maximum aperture of f/2.8. For smaller sensors, the equivalent would be a 10-22mm or 12-24mm zoom.

▶ ▶ ▶ Standard Zooms

This is the range for lenses sold with cameras as a kit. Many versions for consumers and professionals are available. For 35mm, examples are 24-70mm, 28-80mm, and 28-135mm. For digital, 14-54mm, 17-85mm, and 18-70mm are some examples.

▶ ▶ ▶ Telephoto Zooms

The 75-300mm variable aperture lens is the classic consumer telephoto zoom. Many photojournalists have sworn by the constant-f/2.8 80-200mm zoom. A few lenses (e.g., 170-500mm and 80-400mm) reach longer focal lengths. These 35mm lenses are often used on DSLRs as well, where the multiplication of focal length is often favorable. A few telephotos, such as 55-200mm, have been designed specifically for DSLRs.

▶ ▶ ▶ Super or Hyper Zooms

Some zooms have been designed with extensive zoom range, such as 24-200mm, 28-300mm, and 35-350mm. They are meant to be a convenient all-in-one solution to cover most shooting requirements. A digital equivalent would be an 18-125mm or 18-200mm zoom. While one of these lenses can provide the viewing angles of seven prime lenses, the wide zoom range ($7\times$ or more) means that lens designers invariably have to sacrifice something in terms of performance. If you are getting a DSLR for maximum image quality, you might want to consider other lens options.

Attachments

▶ ▶ ▶ Close-Up Lenses

These look more like filters, and they screw onto a normal camera lens in similar fashion. They are an economical way to pursue macro or close-up photography without a dedicated macro lens. Rated in diopters (e.g., +1, +5), they allow you to achieve focus at much closer distances than the actual minimum focus distance of your lens, thereby giving greater magnification. Depending on quality, performance may not quite match up to that of actual macro lenses.

You can even screw on more than one close-up lens at the same time, although the image quality does degrade with this method. Attach the higher diopter lens to the main lens first.

▶ ▶ ▶ Teleconverters (or Extenders)

Using optical elements, these extend the focal length of a lens, but decrease the light entering the lens. A 1.4× teleconverter multiplies the focal length by 1.4, and decreases the light by one stop. A 2× teleconverter doubles the effective focal length, and decreases light by two stops. The camera may not record any change in focal length or effective aperture, but TTL exposure metering will usually ensure a correct exposure anyway.

Unlike close-up lenses, teleconverters do not change the focusing range of a lens. They may therefore be used to photograph distant as well as close subjects. Teleconverters may also degrade image quality, depending on their optical quality.

▲ A teleconverter with electronic lens contacts for communication between camera and lens.

▶ ▶ ▶ Extension Tubes and Bellows

These are basically hollow tubes that allow the lens to be further from the camera body. Extension tubes are rigid, and allow control of the lens via the camera body. They can be stacked to obtain greater extension. Bellows are flexible, accordion-like tubes whose length can be varied precisely, though they are not as convenient for outdoor use. Great degrees of close-up magnification can be obtained depending on the lens used and the amount of extension. Unlike close-up lenses and teleconverters, there are no optical elements to interfere with the image, but note that you will be using your lens outside its normal specifications.

▲ A standard extension tube

▶▶▶ Reversing Rings and Adapters

These are thin metal rings that allow you to attach lenses the other way round, directly to the camera body or to another lens. Depending on the lens used, you can obtain macro shots by doing this. But exercise caution, as you will also be exposing the rear element of the reversed lens to any dust or moisture present.

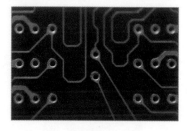

◀ This close-up of a computer circuit board was taken with a reversed 24mm lens. The actual area measures 10mm from left to right. Note the extremely shallow DOF.

10

Using the On-Camera Flash and Flash Modes

While the most expensive DSLRs do not have a built-in pop-up flash to avoid compromising their ruggedness—and perhaps to reinforce the idea that "professionals don't use pop-up flash"—many cameras have one, and you should view it as a convenient tool.

Flash Modes

Built-in flash has a reputation for being harsh, annoying, and producing ugly results. There is a measure of truth in this, but DSLRs usually allow you some measure of control over flash operation, and this makes it easier to get the best results from your pop-up flash.

▶ ▶ ▶ Red-Eye Reduction

Because the pop-up flash is relatively close to the lens, light rays emitted by the flash may reflect off the retinas of your subjects' eyes back into the lens, usually registering in the photo as unnatural red circles in the pupils of the eyes.

To reduce such red-eye effects, many cameras have a red-eye reduction mode. A burst of light is emitted, causing the pupils of the eyes to contract so that less light enters. Unfortunately, the process does slow your shooting down, and also prevents candid shots.

▶ ▶ ▶ Slow-Sync Flash

Slow-sync flash works by using a slow shutter speed in conjunction with flash. This way, the sensor can receive enough light coming from the background while the main subject is correctly exposed by the flash. Without this feature, you might end up with your subject framed against a black background. The main point of caution is that the camera might select a very slow shutter speed, such as 1/4s—too slow for handheld shooting. In such cases, you should steady your camera and inform your subjects to keep very still until you tell them to relax.

Many assume that the picture has been taken once the flash fires, but the exposure is not complete until the shutter closes again.

One workaround for this common problem is to use rear-curtain sync (see below), so that the long exposure occurs before the flash. Another possible solution would be to use normal flash mode in Shutter Priority mode (S or Tv). You can then select a higher shutter speed, such as 1/15s, and see if you can strike a better compromise between preventing motion blur and capturing background illumination.

Either method of selecting a slower shutter speed should produce pleasant effects, but backgrounds lit by fluorescent lighting may give the picture a green cast which is more unsightly than other conditions.

▶ ▶ ▶ Rear-Curtain Sync

Flash normally fires once the shutter opens, at the beginning of the exposure. This is standard front-curtain sync. With long exposures, however, subsequent motion within the scene may be recorded as streaks.

▶ When the subject moves forward after the flash, the streaks appear in front of the initial flash position, which can look unnatural.

Rear-curtain sync fires the flash just before the shutter closes, so that the brightest image is recorded in the final position rather than the starting one.

▶ With rear-curtain sync, the streaks appear more natural, being behind the subject.

Rear-curtain sync is also useful when taking slow shutter-speed shots of people. They will tend to keep still until the flash fires, which in this case correctly signals the end of the exposure.

Flash Output Control

▶ ▶ ▶ TTL Auto or Manual

The easiest way to use built-in flash is in TTL (through-the-lens) auto mode. When you press the shutter release, the camera will emit pre-flashes (weak bursts of flash) to gauge flash output via the exposure meter—before the main flash burst ensues. The camera will ensure that a correct exposure is obtained.

The pop-up flash may also be controlled manually on some cameras. You can choose from full power output, or lower levels. To get a correct exposure, you will need the flash output chart in your camera manual. The variables are flash output level, subject distance, lens aperture, and ISO. This is obviously not an option when you are in a hurry!

▲ Manual flash output menu

▶ ▶ ▶ Flash Exposure Compensation

With flash exposure compensation, the camera adjusts the balance between ambient lighting and light from the flash. You can therefore maintain the overall exposure level, but vary the contribution of the flash. Positive flash exposure compensation increases the visible effect of flash, while negative compensation decreases it.

This is not the same as standard exposure compensation, which can be applied with or without flash. Exposure compensation affects the brightness of the entire photo. Flash exposure compensation only varies the relative strength of the flash. In fact, exposure compensation and flash exposure compensation can be applied simultaneously.

▲ Exposure compensation 0, flash exposure compensation 0

▲ Exposure compensation 0, flash exposure compensation +1

▲ Exposure compensation 0, flash exposure compensation -1

▲ Exposure compensation +1, flash exposure compensation 0

▲ Exposure compensation -1, flash exposure compensation 0

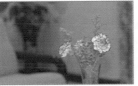

▲ Exposure compensation -1, flash exposure compensation +1

▲ Exposure compensation +1, flash exposure compensation -1

Note that since this feature balances ambient light and flash, it cannot be used correctly when there is insufficient ambient light. There must be at least one other light source.

▶ ▶ ▶ Flash Value Lock

This feature allows you to fire a pre-flash similar to those used in TTL auto mode. By selecting an object of suitable brightness and distance from the camera, you can set the camera to gauge and lock the flash output value. Then, you can point the camera at something else and take a picture, and the flash will fire at the set amount.

This can be used when your subject is very small in the frame, or when it's not placed in the center (which is normally given more importance in exposure calculations).

▶ FV lock on the table beneath the flowers (not in picture) prevented overexposed petals.

Uses for Built-In Flash

▶ ▶ ▶ Fill Flash

Probably the best use for a pop-up flash is daylight fill-in. When sunlight is shining down strongly on faces, harsh shadows are cast under the eyebrows and nose. Sometimes, in backlit situations, the entire front of the person is in shadow, while the background is bright and clear. In other situations, you may find your scene covered by patches of sunlight and shade. While you could expose for either the highlights or the shadows and still get an interesting picture, you may wish to even the scene out.

The built-in flash can be activated in such situations. Using TTL auto mode, the camera will emit enough flash to light up the dark areas while achieving a good balance with the rest of the scene.

One possible problem with fill flash is that the scene may be so bright that the shutter speed needed exceeds the camera's flash sync speed. Adjust your camera settings to decrease the shutter speed: make the aperture smaller, lower the ISO, or add a neutral density filter over your lens (if all else fails).

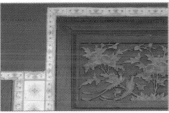 

▲ The exposure is correct, but the colors are a little dull.　　▲ A spot of fill-flash raises the contrast for better colors.

▶ ▶ ▶ Catchlights

Sometimes, your subject may be sufficiently lit, but a bit of pop-up flash can create highlights in the pupils of the eyes (known as catchlights) or on objects in the scene.

▶ ▶ ▶ Color Correction

Another use of pop-up flash is to even out differences in color temperature. You might be photographing a subject under a mix of lighting: a shot indoors under artificial lighting, but with sunlight filtering through a window, for instance. White balance can only neutralize one light source. A bit of flash may help to de-emphasize the color differences of the lighting.

Unorthodox Techniques

To reduce the harshness of built-in flash, you can diffuse the light by holding something over it with your left hand, such as tissue paper or translucent white plastic. This may make the shadows softer, but the exposure may be less accurate. You can also experiment with colored materials or filters to give the flash a color cast.

Whatever you use, keep the object and your fingers from direct contact with the flash tube itself, as it can get quite hot.

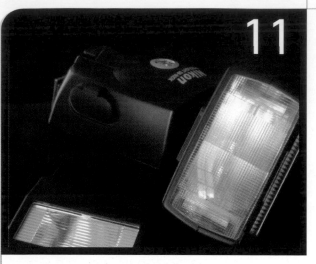

External Flashes and Accessories

Though built-in pop-up flash can be quite useful, its range is limited, and results are not as good as when an external flash is used. Although the basic modes and output controls are similar, an external flash opens up a whole range of possibilities when shooting with flash.

Benefits of External Flash

● **Variable direction**: The greatest benefit of external flash is that you do not have to fire the flash straight at your subject, which can create flat and harsh frontal lighting. By changing the position of the flash unit or the direction of the flashgun head, you can create lighting that is gentler and more naturally contoured.

● **Greater power**: External flash units can light up subjects much farther away than pop-up flash. At the same time, they run on their own power source, and will not drain your camera batteries like the built-in flash. If the flash output per shot is low, the flash recycle time can be much quicker, too.

● **No red-eye effect**: Because the flash is emitted at a greater distance from the lens, direct flash from an external unit enters the subject's eyes from a higher angle and does not reflect back into the lens. You most likely need not waste time and battery power using red-eye reduction.

Flash Output Control

▶ ▶ ▶ Non-TTL Auto

Most external flash units have this mode, in addition to the usual TTL and manual modes. A sensor on the flash unit's body cuts off the flash when it has received enough illumination. This is a less sophisticated method than TTL flash, but it is quite reliable when the scene is of average tone overall.

▶ ▶ ▶ Slave Mode

Some units have the ability to operate as "slave" units: positioned separately from the camera, they fire when the main flash (linked to the camera) fires. You can operate several slave units without using cords. You will need to check for compatibility; when the master flash fires, it may emit pre-flashes that cause the slave units to fire prematurely. In such cases, you may have to switch the master flash to manual mode.

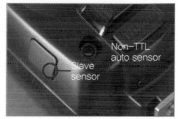

▲ Sensors on a Nikon flash unit

Flash Zoom

This is a worthwhile feature to have, as it adjusts the angle of the flash beam (like a zoom lens) to fit different focal lengths. When the beam is narrowed for longer focal lengths, the light is more concentrated, increasing the range of the flash. The flash may automatically adjust the angle, or you might need to adjust it manually. When setting the zoom angle, use a setting equal to or wider than your lens. If the flash beam is narrower than the view through the lens, the outer edges will not receive any flash. Of course, this effect can be created on purpose for artistic effect.

Bounce Flash

The easiest way to improve flash pictures is to bounce the flash off a ceiling or wall. The flash will light the subject from the top or side, rather than directly in front, producing a more three-dimensional effect. Matte surfaces also diffuse the flash, lighting the scene more softly.

▲ Built-in flash creates flat lighting and casts an unpleasant shadow behind the subject.

▲ Direct external flash is not much better.

▲ Bounce flash is much softer, though the eyes are in shadow.

Choose a white or neutral surface, otherwise the flash will light your subject with a color cast. Aim the flash at a point on the ceiling or wall midway between the flash and the subject. If the subject is close, point the flash straight up. If the flash is aimed too far forward from the flash, the light will bounce down behind the subject instead.

Avoid bouncing the flash where there are lighting fixtures or other reflective objects. These can reflect the flash and create a pattern on your subject. Also be aware of the range of your flash. If the ceiling is too high, the flash may not be able to reach the ceiling and travel all the way back down again to light your subject. In such cases, use direct flash.

A well-known technique is to use a reflector card in conjunction with bounce flash. You can attach either a homemade or commercially produced card to the flash head. When the flash fires upward, some of the light hits the card and reflects straight at the subject, filling in some of the shadows the bounced flash creates. This can also be used when the ceiling is too high up to reflect bounced light.

▲ A small built-in reflector card on a flash head

▲ LumiQuest 80-20

▲ A white card has filled in the shadows while the bounce flash gives overall lighting.

Bounce flash is best used in TTL or non-TTL auto modes. If you are using manual mode, note that the distance should be calculated based on the path of the flash to the bounce surface and then to the subject. Do not simply measure the physical distance between the flash unit and subject.

Off-Camera Flash

Another way to get better flash results is to use the flash off-camera. A sync cord allows you to control the flash at a distance from the camera. You can then light your subject from other directions than the camera position. This is not just for portraiture; it is often used in close-up insect photography, for example.

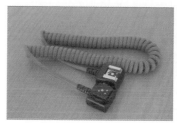

▲ Nikon TTL sync cord

▶ Off-camera flash can be harsh, but the effect is different from direct on-camera flash.

Flash Attachments

▶ ▶ ▶ Diffusers

Usually made of translucent plastic, diffusers serve to soften the effect of flash by scattering the light rays in different directions. At the same time, they do reduce the effective range of the flash.

Diffusers come in various shapes and sizes. In addition to those created by the manufacturer of the flash unit, third-party designs are available in standard and specialized forms. You can often purchase diffusers made specifically for your flash model.

▲ Snap-on diffuser

▲ Direct flash, undiffused

▲ Direct flash, diffused

▶ ▶ ▶ Extenders

Nature photographers, especially those who photograph birds and animals in shade or trees, benefit from using fill flash outdoors. Lenses above 300mm are often used, since many creatures are photographed from a distance. But most flash heads only zoom to about 105mm, and have insufficient range. Flash extenders focus the flash beams to an even tighter angle, allowing a greater flash range.

▲ The product shown is the Visual Echoes Flash Extender also marketed as the Better Beamer, designed by Walt Anderson.

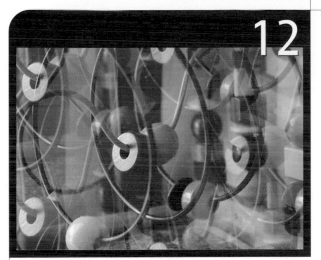

12

Filters

Some may think that digital white balance makes filters (lens attachments that alter the light that passes through the lens) redundant. While white balance is indeed an excellent color adjustment method, some filters remain very relevant to digital photography. Those who have an extensive filter collection—and the know-how to use them —need not abandon them.

Polarizing Filters

Polarizing filters are very useful for deepening the blue of skies and accentuating clouds. Rotate them in their ring or holder till you obtain the effect you want.

These filters are also useful for controlling reflections. Rotating them will alternately increase and decrease the strength of reflections. You may be able to take better shots through glass this way, for instance.

Most DSLRs will need circular polarizing filters rather than the linear type. Linear polarizing filters may cause errors with exposure metering.

▲ The side table shows reflections on its varnished surface.   ▲ A polarizing filter can minimize reflections.

Graduated Filters

This is another useful type of filter for digital photography. Part of the filter is gray (or another tone), and the color gradually turns clear across the filter. If the transition is very gradual, it is called a soft grad; if the transition is more abrupt, it is a hard grad. Hard and soft grads are also available in a variety of tones, usually categorized by the number of stops of light they block.

Graduated filters are used mainly to decrease the brightness of part of the scene (usually the sky), so that the contrast range of the whole scene is reduced. Thus, you will be able to retain better detail in the darker regions, while the brighter parts will not be overexposed.

▲ This exposure is acceptable, but the brightness of the sky pushes the trees into the darker tones.

▲ With a graduated filter, the morning sun on the treetops is captured more accurately.

Color Correction Filters

Many digital photographers do not see a need for these, since they can correct color temperature in tungsten or fluorescent lighting using white balance. Still, color correction filters can be used, except that you will have to abandon auto WB—it will attempt to cancel the filter's effect. If your filters are made for use with daylight-balanced film, set the camera to daylight or sunny WB.

For filters that are used to warm up or cool down the color temperature, you may set custom WB first, and then attach the filter. But if you only have a filter intended for the effect opposite to the effect you desire, do the opposite: attach the filter when setting custom WB, and remove it before shooting. For example, if you set custom WB using a light blue filter, removing the filter will create a warming effect in your pictures.

Special Effects Filters

Quite a few filter effects can be simulated by computer software, so you may not need to purchase them. On the other hand, you may wish to create diffusion or star-burst effects in-camera, and there are indeed many different options available to you.

Infrared Filters

Some DSLR sensors are sensitive to infrared (IR) light, and can be used for IR photography. To find out if yours is capable of this, take a photo of an infrared source, such as a remote control, in a dim environment. If you can see a bright spot emitted by the device, your camera does record IR.

Filters for IR photography are virtually opaque; they only let invisible IR beams through. As a result, you will not be able to look through the viewfinder while the filter is on. Focusing is also difficult; infrared light does not focus at the same point as visible light, so you cannot follow the distance scale exactly. Some lenses have an IR focusing mark to help you.

Screw-In vs. Holder

Round, screw-in filters are very common. When attached to a lens, they do not add much to the its bulk. They also cover the front element completely and thus offer some protection.

▲ Cokin filter holder and grad

Some filter systems, such as the Cokin and Lee systems, use rectangular filters placed in a holder mounted on the lens. Changing filters is very easy as you just have to slide them in and out. Extra-large filters and holders are available for wide-angle lenses, to avoid vignetting of the image.

Holder systems are more unwieldy and bulky, but are better for graduated filters, since you can adjust the critical point of graduation. Some screw-in graduated filters place the transition right in the middle, which does not suit many landscape compositions. The same applies for the positioning of soft-focus or vignetting filter effects. Slide-in filters would be better in these scenarios.

Step-Up Rings

Apart from a basic UV filter to protect the front element, you may not want to purchase filters for every diameter of lens you own. Even a moderate collection of lenses could have five different filter sizes. If you wish to share filters between your lenses, you can purchase filters for the largest diameter lens you own (or plan to purchase). This could be 77mm or 82mm. Then, buy step-up rings to fit the smaller lenses to the filters. The disadvantage is that a large filter may be quite cumbersome on a small lens.

▲ Step-up rings

13

Shooting Indoors

We have covered many areas relating to the functions of cameras, lenses, and flash. Before going on to focus on some specific photographic subjects, we will first cover the general techniques you'll need to know to shoot indoors and outdoors with a DSLR. This section introduces some factors to be considered in indoor situations.

Artificial Lighting

Although DSLRs have more sophisticated and reliable WB than compact digital cameras, their Auto WB performance is usually less effective indoors. Compared with natural light, artificial lighting is usually dimmer, its color temperature varies widely depending on the light source, and some types flicker, resulting in photos with inconsistent brightness or color temperature.

▶ ▶ ▶ Use Presets with Fine-Tuning

If Auto WB does not give good results, the first option you have is to use WB fine-tuning, possibly with a camera preset. Sometimes, all you need is to fine-tune the Auto WB in the right direction. Otherwise, you may have to choose a preset such as Incandescent/Tungsten or Fluorescent, and fine-tune or bracket WB from the basic setting. Even the Sunny/Daylight setting

▲ Auto WB does a reasonable job in this situation.

▲ Incandescent/Tungsten makes the scene less yellow.

suits some artificial lighting. When you hit on a good WB, you can set custom WB using that image.

Chapter 2

The main thing is to develop an eye for color temperature, which does take experience. Use the LCD review to gauge the effects of different settings.

▶ ▶ ▶ Custom WB

This is the next option, a convenient one if you are able to get either your neutral card or your camera into a position where it receives illumination that is representative of the lighting of your scene. If you are close to your subject, you can easily set custom WB. If you are rather far away, though, another option would be to temporarily use a lens with a longer focal length to isolate a neutral area in the distant scene as a custom WB sample.

◀ The central pillar in the background—used to set custom WB—is now (inaccurately) neutral gray

Mixed Lighting

Another challenge you'll face when shooting in artificial light is that the scene might be illuminated by daylight as well as artificial light, or by more than one type of artificial lighting. This makes it difficult to maintain a consistent color temperature. For instance, one side of a person's face might be lit differently than the other. However, there are steps you can take to improve the situation.

▲ Auto WB does not give a good result for this mixture of incandescent and fluorescent lighting.

▲ This portrait, taken under mixed indoor and window light with Auto WB, is not ideal either.

▶ ▶ ▶ Remove Secondary Sources

You might be able to change the lighting by simply drawing the blinds or curtains, or by changing position and shooting from another direction. If you're photographing people, you can get your subjects to move away from sources of unwanted light.

▶ Left: Shooting from another angle excludes most of the fluorescent light and improves color, but not the background.

▶ ▶ Right: Having the subject face away from the window removes most of the effects of window light.

▶ ▶ ▶ Set WB for Dominant Source

If most of your subject is under just one kind of lighting, you can set WB for the dominant light source. If you are setting custom WB, face your card toward the main light only. The results of this technique will be somewhat unpredictable, since you're not accounting for secondary light sources. You'll have to judge for yourself whether the WB you get is acceptable.

▲ Setting custom WB for the incandescent results in pale, cold skin tones on the right side.

▲ Setting custom WB for the fluorescent results in a reddish hue on the left of the face and neck.

▲ Setting custom WB for window light makes the left of the subject too orange.

▲ Setting custom WB for the indoor lighting leaves the right side too cool in tone.

▶ ▶ ▶ Set WB to Average

If the lighting mix from the different sources is even, you can set WB to average the effects of the combined lighting. There could be two or more secondary color casts on the edges of your subject or scene, but they will not be so apparent. To set custom WB, place your card so that it is evenly lit by the different sources. If you are using a flexible card, you could try curving the card so that it gets better exposure from different angles.

▲ Taking a reference shot on location, using an object of known color, enables you to be more precise when making corrections on your computer.

▲ For the best overall color, be sure to include both light sources.

▲ Again, both light sources are accounted for.

▶ ▶ ▶ Use Flash

You can overpower artificial lighting if your flash is strong enough. At distances up to a few yards, the camera's built-in flash should suffice, but at greater distances you'll need an external unit. Set WB to Auto or Flash, because you are now using flash as your main light source. Do not use slow-sync flash mode for this purpose.

▶ When flash is stronger than ambient light, Flash WB gives correct color.

Balancing Flash Output

Indoor light levels are sometimes so low that a high ISO (e.g., 1600) is required to photograph without flash. The resulting pictures may exhibit excessive noise, so it's good to use flash to provide more light, enabling you to use lower ISOs (such as 400).

▲ At ISO 400, the subject is underexposed without flash.

▲ Spot-metering the face improves the picture, but subject contrast is low, and the fountain is overexposed.

Using flash and lower ISOs will successfully light up your subject, but not necessarily the background. A lower ISO has less sensitivity to light, and flash has a limited range; in a large hall, for instance, you may find that the background of a flash photo turns out too dark (or totally black).

In this section, we'll explore your options for creating balanced lighting while using flash.

▲ Normal flash mode is quite acceptable for this mid-range scene.

▶ ▶ ▶ Using Slow-Sync Flash to Achieve Balanced Lighting

Slow-sync flash mode is one method of balancing flash and background illumination. However, the camera mode you select will have an effect on its functionality.

If you use Program (P) mode, the camera will automatically balance flash power, shutter speed, and aperture. If you use Aperture Priority (A/Av) mode, you can choose the aperture and control depth-of-field.

▲ Slow-sync flash shows the background just a little bit more.

In both cases, you have to keep an eye on the shutter speed, which may be very slow. The shutter is open for longer than the duration of the flash, allowing ambient lighting to affect your results. Also, slower shutter speeds create more opportunities for camera or subject movement to cause blurring. Be sure to steady the camera on a tripod or other firm support.

Another way to balance indoor illumination is to use Shutter Priority (S/Tv) mode. If the camera is handheld, set the shutter speed to 1/30s or slower, depending on how steady you can hold the camera and whether your subjects are moving. On some cameras, the viewfinder displays the degree of underexposure. You can use this information to gauge how much darker the background might turn out, but realize that this also depends on how much the flash brightens the background.

▲ A shutter speed of 1/15s allows you to use a smaller aperture, increasing DOF in the background.

▲ An extra-slow shutter speed of 1/2s has smoothened the water flow, while the flash helps to reduce visible camera shake.

Alternatively, you can shoot in Manual (M) mode. Set a slow shutter speed and set the aperture to yield an appropriate DOF. Look at the exposure display to gauge the level of background underexposure; the reading should be less than -1 if you want the background to be clearly visible. Adjust the shutter speed or aperture until you get an acceptable exposure level.

▶ ▶ ▶ Flash Exposure Compensation
If your camera offers this flash control, you can use it to adjust the contribution of the flash to the overall exposure. In particular, it affects the color temperature balance between flash and ambient light on your main subject.

▶ ▶ ▶ WB Setting

When used to balance ambient light, flash becomes one of the light sources, and not necessarily the main one. As a result, using Flash WB may not give desirable results. Depending on the flash output level, you might need to treat the situation as a mixed-lighting scene, and set WB taking into account the existing light sources as well as the flash.

▲ Flash WB on a long exposure gives a reddish result here due to the influence of ambient light.

ℝeflections

Glass and mirrors are common in urban indoor settings. Sometimes, they can create opportunities for interesting compositions. However, you always need to be on the lookout for unwanted reflections and bright spots caused by flash.

▶ ▶ ▶ Reducing Reflections

When shooting through glass, the first thing you can do to minimize unwanted reflections is to move the front of your lens as close to the glass as possible. It may help to hold the camera with one hand and shade it with the other.

▲ Note the distracting reflections in this picture.

▲ Moving in close and shading with a hand cuts the reflections out.

When shooting through glass at an angle, you can use a polarizing filter. Rotate the polarizer until you obtain the best effect.

▶ A polarizing filter helps reduce reflections.

▶ ▶ ▶ Flash Reflections

When you shoot with flash, your flash unit becomes a very bright light source. If flash is reflected directly into the camera lens by glass or mirrors, it might cause a white "hot spot," or its brightness might cause the whole scene to be wrongly exposed. For this example, a mirror-lined elevator is used to exaggerate the effect of flash reflections.

▲ Directly reflected flash creates a bright white spot.

▲ Shooting at an angle to the glass removes direct reflections, though in this case secondary reflections are visible all around.

The easiest solution is to shoot at an angle to the glass or mirrors; hopefully, this will prevent the flash from reflecting back in your direction. If the ceiling is suitable, you can also bounce the flash.

In the unlikely situation that you cannot avoid shooting straight at a mirror, position yourself so that the subject blocks the image of the flash in the mirror. If your flash unit is higher than your subject, you may need to stoop a little.

▲ Bouncing light upwards rather than at the mirror creates a better lighting effect, although the diffuser still causes a hot spot.

▲ Hiding the flash behind the subject stops most of the flash reflections.

14

Shooting Outdoors

We'll now turn our attention to outdoor photography. Almost any type of photography can be performed outdoors, and indeed some specializations are strictly outdoor activities. This section will be generally applicable to most photography in the open.

Preparing to Shoot Outdoors

If you are going to be out for a considerable period of time, and your destination is not near supplies of some sort, you should prepare by making a list of the equipment you'll need and checking that your equipment is working properly. Battery power is particularly crucial for DSLRs, as well as flash units, so make sure you take enough batteries with you.

When the light levels are low, or when you want to maximize DOF, you will need a steady support for your camera. Ideally you will have a tripod or monopod with you, but this may not be practical in all circumstances. The best substitute is a beanbag, which is compact and can be molded to fit your camera and lens snugly. You can also use extra items of clothing for this purpose, but the support will not be quite as firm.

In the field, you may be at the mercy of the elements, so make sure your equipment is well protected. If your bag is not water-resistant, carry plastic bags with watertight seals to wrap your equipment in. Be careful in dusty or sandy places: Tiny specks can invade crevices and jam mechanisms, or get into the camera lens mount when you change lenses. Try to minimize the camera's exposure to harmful particles and sea spray. Also, you should consider carrying a basic cleaning kit that includes a blower bulb and a soft lens brush or lens tissue. Cleaning equipment outdoors is inconvenient, but may sometimes be unavoidable.

One old technique for protecting the camera while shooting in unfavorable conditions is to seal it in a plastic bag. Start by placing the camera in the bag, but leave the lens filter off. Then, carefully screw on the filter so that it cuts the plastic along the filter groove. Unscrew the filter, remove the cut-out circle, and replace the filter—with the plastic bag still in the lens screw thread. Unfortunately, it is not easy to seal the camera this way; further, it can be difficult to operate the camera controls through the plastic.

Shooting in Sunlight

▶ ▶ ▶ Practical Considerations

Camera equipment can get very hot under strong sunlight, especially if your camera is black. Keep your equipment away from direct sunlight as much as possible.

When shooting under bright sunlight, it can be hard to see through the viewfinder. Wearing a cap or hat to shade your eyes will help. Using your LCD is much more problematic: You may not be able to view pictures or access menus without moving into the shade. Adjusting the brightness of your LCD may help, but if you do so, remember that what you see there may not accurately reflect the pictures you're taking. Use the histogram as a more accurate gauge of exposure.

▶ Use your hand to keep extraneous light out.

▶ ▶ ▶ Quality of Light

The word "photography" comes from the Greek words for "light" and "writing," and it is the quality of the light that is written or recorded to an image file that determines the quality of the photographs we take. The following series of photographs shows the quality of light at different hours of the day.

▲ Just before 7 AM

▲ At about 10:30 AM

▲ At about 1 PM

▲ At 6 PM

▲ Just before 7 PM

▶ ▶ ▶ Color Temperature

Natural light varies in color temperature throughout the day. It also makes a difference whether the subject—or scene—is in direct sunlight or in the shade. In particular, the hours just after dawn and just before sundown are sometimes called the "golden hours" because of the attractive "golden" rays of the sun low in the sky.

When you want the color of light to be reproduced as seen, set your WB so the color is retained rather than neutralized. If you want to make the color cast different from the actual scene, set a WB appropriate for that purpose.

▲ As shown in these photos, all taken within one minute, the same scene can be given a cold or warm tint using WB settings.

▶ ▶ ▶ Direction of Light

The angle of the sun's rays varies with the time of day, and to a lesser extent with the time of year. The orientation of your subject determines how shadows will be cast. If your subject is immovable, like the house above, different surfaces will be directly illuminated at different hours. You might wish to use a map or compass to assess the best time to photograph a scene or monument from a certain direction.

If you are photographing people, be especially careful about shadows cast on faces. Eyes may be lost in shadow under the brow, and noses may project long shapes over the lips. If possible, move people into the shade, where light is not strongly directional. If not, try turning them to face a better direction with respect to the light. If necessary, use fill flash to lighten shadow areas.

▲ Front lighting is easy to understand and use, and provides good color and contrast.

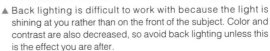

▲ Side lighting highlights edges and gives definition. It can enhance the feeling of three-dimensionality.

▲ Back lighting is difficult to work with because the light is shining at you rather than on the front of the subject. Color and contrast are also decreased, so avoid back lighting unless this is the effect you are after.

▶ ▶ ▶ Intensity of Light

Looking again at the series of house photos, we can see that natural light varies not just in color and direction, but in intensity. Light can also be hard or soft in its effect. Hard light (such as direct sunlight) is strongly directional and produces shadows with defined edges, while soft light (such as that diffused through clouds or reflected from another direction) illuminates from several angles and produces gentler gradations.

Light can be strong or weak in brightness. Strong, hard light gives higher contrast and vivid colors, but too high a contrast range may be difficult or impossible for a digital sensor to fully record. In such situations, you can try some of the following:

- Set the contrast or tone parameter to the lowest setting.
- Use a polarizing filter to lighten the shadow areas.
- Use fill flash to lighten shadows (if they are within flash range).
- Shoot in RAW format and fine-tune the image on your computer using RAW adjustment software.
- Take two photos—one exposed for the highlights and one for the shadows—using a tripod to maintain exactly the same camera position. Then combine the two images on your computer.

▲ Normal contrast   ▲ The low contrast setting improves shadow detail just a bit.   ▲ A polarizer reduces the shadows.

Controlling Depth-of-Field

Maximizing depth-of-field is especially important in landscape photography. Conversely, portraits often use shallow DOF to focus attention on the subject. Normally, when you look through the viewfinder, you are seeing the scene through the lens at maximum aperture. This ensures a bright view and aids autofocus, but does not allow you to gauge what the DOF is going to be if you shoot at a smaller aperture. Some DSLRs have a DOF preview function, which lets you see the effective DOF through the viewfinder, before the photo is taken. This is done by temporarily adjusting the lens to the set aperture. However, at small apertures the viewfinder may become too dark for you to estimate DOF.

A slightly more roundabout method is to use the LCD review to gauge DOF. By magnifying the image on screen, you can see more clearly where the zone of apparent sharpness extends. Scroll around the image to see areas at different distances.

If you want to maximize DOF but have no suitable DOF scale or table, you can use hyperfocal focusing. First, set the aperture you want to use. Next, focus at infinity or the far point in your photo. Now use DOF preview, or take a picture at infinity focus and review the image; the aim is to find the nearest point that is acceptably sharp. Finally, refocus the lens at the identified distance and take the picture. The DOF should range from before the focus point all the way to infinity.

▲ The series of photos to the right reflects the image quality at the focal points shown above.

▲ With the focus at infinity, the DOF does not extend to the nearest part of the picture.

▲ With the focus on the nearest pillar, the DOF suffers at greater distances.

▲ Refocusing to the nearest sharp point extends DOF to cover nearly the whole scene.

40 Digital SLR Techniques

Photographing People and Sports

People as subjects are often the most fascinating and difficult to capture in photography. Besides fussing over the usual things, such as focus, exposure, lighting, placement, and color, a good portrait photographer must be able to capture the character and personality of the person in the shot.

For novice photographers, taking photos of family and friends is the easiest and most rewarding way to start photographing people. In this chapter, let's begin by learning to take photos of your loved ones and the people around you.

Having covered the basics of photographing people, we'll move on to cover the fast-paced world of sports photography, which has its own set of unique demands.

15 Studio Photography

Digital cameras have made studio photography easier to learn and set up, especially for beginners. The main advantages relate to white balance and the instant feedback of the LCD screen. With adjustable white balance, you can fine tune to get neutral lighting either on the camera itself or while processing raw images. Checking your results on the LCD panel allows you to make changes to lighting arrangements without having to use polaroids (a common practice when working with film cameras). In the following section, we'll review the basics of studio photography.

Studio Equipment

▶ ▶ ▶ Background

This is perhaps the simplest of all the components of a studio set. The color and size of your backdrop depends on your subject and the end product of your image. If you are shooting a head-and-shoulder portrait, you may not need a large backdrop, just one sufficient to fill your frame. However, if you are shooting a full-length portrait or a product photo to be used in a catalog, you may consider getting a paper or muslin cloth backdrop that is seamless–to disguise the line between the wall and floor. An even-colored backdrop is useful for catalog products, as it's easier to isolate the product from the background later (like blue-screening in movies). Common colors for starters are white, gray, and black.

▶ ▶ ▶ Camera Settings

Your main concern in a studio situation is white balance. While it is acceptable to set your camera to auto white balance, a better method is to custom white balance your camera to suit your flash lighting. You may use a white card or a gray card as a target to set the white balance. See Chapter 1 for further details.

You can set the aperture by taking a few shots and evaluating the histogram. Remember, the shutter speed controls the amount of ambient light and will not affect the exposure on a subject lit by studio lights. Just be sure to use a shutter speed equal to or slower than your flash sync speed to avoid having a dark band on your image.

▶ ▶ ▶ Lighting

Why do you need studio lighting? Just two reasons: versatility and control. Once you set up the lights, the results will be very predictable. Straight-on camera flash may produce red-eye and unflattering, flat lighting. Background shadows may also be too intense. Studio lights can be arranged to provide side lighting that gives a more flattering 3D effect.

Studio lighting can be classified under continuous light and flash. Continuous lighting is a good way to start if you have a small budget. However, it generally produces more heat and is not daylight-balanced. There is nothing much you can do to remedy the heat generation, but to overcome color temperature issues, shoot in RAW mode and adjust your photos later on a computer to get the correct or most pleasing color temperature. Any lamp can be used as a continuous light source, although you will likely want to soften the light by diffusing it with tracing paper or a thin cloth.

Flash refers to on-camera flash or studio flash. For flash, you won't know beforehand what the effect of the lighting will be. However, studio flash features continuous lamps to show you the lighting effect before the flash fires. This is called modeling light. Although these "sample" lights are lower powered compared to the flash itself, you will learn to judge the effect through practice. Studio flash is daylight-balanced and you can achieve consistent color temperature.

For most home users, studio lights in the range of 300-600 watt-seconds should suffice. Watt-seconds, or joules, are used to measure the power that a flash can produce.

▲ A 500 W·s light with an umbrella attached.

Accessories

Light from a bare flash is raw in that there is little control over the quality of the light. Accessories are used to control light in a studio. Common accessories include softboxes, umbrellas, and reflectors.

▶ ▶ ▶ Softbox

To get nice, soft lighting, use a softbox. A softbox is a larger light source that forces light through a fabric diffuser to reduce the harsh shadows created by a bare lamp. The effect is more pleasing, with less-defined shadows.

▲ This picture was taken with a softbox and a silver reflector to lighten the shadows.

▶ ▶ ▶ Umbrella

Umbrellas make the source of light larger, and therefore softer, much like a softbox. However, because a softbox surrounds the flash, it doesn't lose as much light as an umbrella. Umbrellas come with white, silver, and translucent layers:

- A white layer gives a soft, diffused light, and is good for general purpose use.
- A silver layer gives a "harder" light and is common when shooting glamour.
- A translucent layer can be used as a diffuser, much like the softbox. Many umbrellas have a reflective layer, which can be removed to expose a translucent layer for "shoot-through" lighting.

▲ Umbrellas also make the light source softer.

▶ ▶ ▶ Reflector

Reflectors come in different colors: white, silver, gold, or translucent. Most reflectors offer a combination of colors for you to choose from for different situations. A gold reflector provides "warm," reflected light. White, silver, and translucent reflectors give the same effect as the corresponding umbrella.

Reflectors are used to cut down shadows from the lights and give a more even lighting effect.

With a combination of studio lights, softbox, umbrella, and reflector, you will be able to get consistent lighting, which you have full control over.

▲ A silver reflector

Chapter 3

16

Weddings

Sometimes you may be asked by family members or friends to photograph their weddings. While it may seem daunting at first, there are a few important techniques you can pick up to help you face this challenge.

Preparation

It pays to be prepared by checking all your equipment the day before the wedding. Check to make sure that the batteries are fully charged, memory cards are formatted and sufficient for the event, lenses are cleaned, and the flash and camera are functioning. Make a checklist to ensure you have all the equipment you need packed in the bag.

Always scope out the wedding first by arriving early (if pre-wedding reconnaissance is not possible). This will allow you to familiarize yourself with the location and its lighting conditions.

Technique

▶ ▶ ▶ Aperture and Shutter Speed Selection

Try to keep your aperture at f/4 for individual portraits (to throw the background out of focus), and f/8 when shooting large groups. The f/8 setting will give you more depth-of-field to ensure the different "layers" of people remain sharp. When shooting indoors, beware of shutter speeds dropping too low for handheld photography if you are not using a flash.

As a guide, the minimum shutter speed should be the reciprocal of your lens. For example, if you use a 200mm lens, avoid using a shutter speed slower than 1/200s.

▲ An aperture of f/8 was selected to ensure that everyone remains sharp.

▲ For this individual portrait, an aperture of f/4 was selected to throw the background out of focus.

▶ ▶ ▶ Lens Choice

For portraits, use a standard or telephoto lens that ranges from 50mm and 150mm. Prime lenses or fixed focal length lenses are perfect for this, too, as they are sharp and focus quickly. For big groups, use a wide-angle lens if necessary, but be careful to avoid distortion at the edges. Keep lens changing to a minimum to avoid wasting time and getting dust onto your camera's sensor.

▶ ▶ ▶ Flash

If you are using flash indoors, you will get softer and more flattering lighting if you bounce your flash off a reflector or the ceiling. Bouncing requires you to tilt the flash 45 degrees or more into a reflector or the ceiling. If you are using the ceiling to bounce, be careful if the color isn't white; it might apply a color cast to your shots. Don't be afraid to "drag" the shutter by using a lower shutter speed, say 1/30s. This allows more ambient light to be captured to preserve the mood of the place. You can also create artistic shots with blurred backgrounds.

▲ A slow shutter speed of 1/20s was used to allow the background to blur.

● Indoor Shooting with Flash

If there is a lot of available light streaming in from windows and doorways, take a meter reading of the outside light and set the aperture on the camera accordingly to expose for the outside light. Modern flashes with TTL (through-the-lens) metering will ensure that the subject is exposed properly. The balance between outside light and the flash will make the result look more natural. Flash also freezes fast action–very useful for the more photojournalistic style of pictures.

▲ Flash freezes the petals as they were tossed.

● Outdoor Shooting with Flash

Many people think that shooting outdoors does not require flash, but using fill-in flash will lift the shadows caused by harsh sunlight. The fill-in flash will also lighten dark eye sockets and give a more pleasing result.

Ⓦhat to Shoot

Here are some suggestions of what to shoot on the wedding day itself. The list is by no means comprehensive, but it should serve as a general guide:

1. The church interior and exterior
2. The reception table
3. The wedding party, including families, bridal party, groomsmen, etc.
4. The processional
5. The presentation of the bride by her father
6. The wedding service itself (try to avoid flash photography if possible)
7. The signing of the marriage certificate (if applicable)
8. The recessional
9. The mingling of guests outside
10. The party/reception
11. Candid shots of guests at their tables
12. The bouquet toss
13. The cutting of the cake

14. The couple's first dance
15. The minor details of the scene: signs, the program, decorations, etc.
16. The departure of the happy couple

▲ An example of details to look out for.

Final Words

Bring plenty of batteries and memory cards. These are relatively cheap compared to the priceless pictures you will miss if you run out. Practice beforehand, and not during the wedding, if you are unsure of certain techniques. And, lastly, have fun; weddings are, after all, joyous occasions.

17

Photographing Children

Childhood, while magical and fleeting, is also a time of constant action and spontaneity. Treat a photo session with kids as a time for fun and games, and go with the flow. The results may differ from what you initially planned, but you could get some great shots nevertheless.

Camera Settings

Children can be constantly active. Keeping them in sharp focus may prove to be a challenge. If their movement is somewhat repetitive, you can pre-focus using one-shot AF. With the focus locked, you will be ready to fire the shutter when your subject reaches the desired position. If the children are running all over, though, you might try continuous AF, or if that fails, switch to MF. This way, you can compose the picture without having to keep an AF point on your subject's eyes all the time.

If actions and poses are changing all the time, you could try continuous shooting. It may increase your chances of capturing a good expression or position. This is likely to be a more feasible option with JPEG rather than RAW images, though.

To maintain a shutter speed fast enough to freeze the action, try a setting of around ISO 400, and adjust according to the lighting. Set a suitable shutter speed using S/Tv mode, or set a larger aperture in A/Av mode. If using flash, do not exceed the camera's flash sync speed. Alternatively, use a slow shutter speed and pan the camera to match the action.

Babies' eyes are rather sensitive, so you should not use direct flash closer than one meter (about three feet). Instead, use bounced flash if you want to shoot from close up, or use a longer focal length to allow for direct flash at a greater distance.

Chapter 3

Working with Babies and Toddlers

From birth to two or three months, young infants generally do not smile. They sometimes do approximate a smile, but this is more like a reflex and not something you can coax from them. You can photograph young babies awake, or asleep, with their accompanying expressions. Their necks are not strong, so make sure their heads are supported at all times.

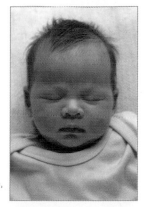

▶ Newborns are asleep much of the time, but they are endearing nevertheless.

Infants need to be fed and changed often, so be sensitive to their needs and those of the parents. Be flexible and make the most of the situation if things do not go as planned. When a photo opportunity arises, seize it and work quickly.

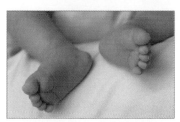

▲ Tiny toes (and other details) can still be photographed when the baby is asleep.

It would be natural to involve the baby's parents in the shot. They can be included in the photo, where you can capture their parental love and pride, or they can help support the baby while remaining out of the frame.

▲ Father and daughter make for a delightful image.

▲ This family portrait makes use of the differences in size to tell its story.

Older babies and toddlers do smile in response to attractive objects, sounds, or funny faces. They have really lovely smiles; at younger ages they will beam at almost anyone or anything, but when older they may take time to warm up to strangers. Some babies and toddlers might be inseparable from their parents.

▶ Babies adore their parents, so ask the parents to amuse them from outside the frame.

You may find that babies will smile at you, but once you bring up the camera, the smile turns to a quizzical stare. One trick you can try is to play peek-a-boo using the DSLR. Bring the camera to your eye for brief moments, maintaining eye contact with the baby in-between. Lock the focus in one of these moments. Then, when you get the baby to smile, quickly raise the camera and take the picture without delay.

▲ This photo was taken using the above method.

▲ Pre-focusing was used to snap this shot once the windows opened.

To get a closer, more engaged shot, you should get down to their level, both physically and mentally. Shooting from a lower viewpoint enables you to photograph babies' and children's faces more clearly. Also try to relate to them as people, just as you would for a portrait session with adults. Your interaction might be limited, but the effort will definitely improve your photos.

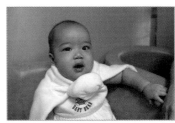
▲ Shooting at eye level gives a better baby portrait.

▲ Taking the effort to relate to toddlers allows them to be more relaxed with you.

◀ Try to see the world from their point of view.

In this period of "firsts," babies will first sit up, then crawl, then pull themselves to standing position, and finally begin walking. These are important stages that can be photographed if you're lucky. They may have very short attention spans, so you will have to be quick, since they may not demonstrate their new skills more than a few times. You may also have to give them something to occupy themselves with, in order to stave off boredom or impatience.

▲ Toddlers are curious about everything; often, you can photograph them when they are absorbed in doing something.

▲ Be quick to capture anything funny or unusual.

Working with Children

By the time they are a few years old, young children will be running, talking, and possibly making things difficult for everyone around them. They also may have learned to smile "for the camera," sometimes resulting in artificial expressions. But their abilities and personalities are blooming and there will be lots of different photo possibilities. When working with them, it's probably better to involve them in some kind of game than try to direct their behavior.

If you want to take formal or semi-formal portraits, you can set up a mini-studio. Studio or hotshoe-mounted flash may be useful to freeze movement, especially if the children are active. If you are taking candid shots, however, it is probably best not to use flash (to avoid unnatural lighting). Let the children begin an activity, then be patient. Start shooting to get them used to you and they should gradually become accustomed to your presence and even forget about it.

▶ Bubbles are sure to delight most children; all the better if you can make a game out of it.

With older children, you could try a more conventional approach, though their attention span and patience might still be limited. They will understand better what a photo session is, and may thus be more cooperative. You can help them feel more comfortable by being friendly and explaining what effect or look you are trying to achieve. They will be excited to see the pictures you have taken on the LCD display, so be sure to share the process with them.

▲ Shooting from their eye level is still a good idea.

▲ Children soon learn what cameras are for.

▲ If you wait, the children may eventually ignore you.

◀ Be creative! Just saying "Smilee!" doesn't work so well sometimes.

Photographing Children in Public

In street photography, children have been common subjects as they are often at play, and are also generally keener to be photographed than adults. Many classic shots document the lives of children through the twentieth century, and capture the timelessness of childhood while creating a historical record.

▲ Young chess addicts on the subway

Times have changed, however, and photographing other people's children can be threatening to their parents or other observers. In some countries, the police have questioned photographers and inspected their pictures on suspicion of perverse motives.

▲ Bright colors on a gray day

▲ A bizarre version of the tooth fairy perhaps?

▲ This bench seats three.

You obviously need to be aware of what is acceptable socially when taking photos outside. In any case, go about your photography openly. Hold your camera in plain sight rather than tucking it away in your bag. Ask for permission to shoot, from your intended subjects or any accompanying adults, and be prepared to explain your actions if asked. It's relatively easy to do so with the image review on the LCD.

18

Sports Photography

We are all fascinated by action shots, especially those that capture the peak of excitement in sports. Several factors need to come together for you to get good sports shots. In this chapter, we will review methods for getting solid results.

Knowledge of the Sport

Although not a necessity, it will be advantageous if you are familiar with the specific sport you're set to photograph. This will help in predicting the action that is about to happen.

▶ ▶ ▶ Location

Knowing where to locate yourself will contribute greatly to the success of your shot(s). You should not only be concerned with the subject, but also the background. Position yourself such that the background does not distract the viewer from the subject. Fill the frame with your subject as much as possible. Most people will not have a press pass to get right in the action, so try to get as close as possible.

▶ The busy background in the picture is blurred using an aperture of f/2.8 to isolate the subject from the background.

Chapter 3

quipment

Since you are limited to shooting from a distance most of the time, having a telephoto lens is a necessity. Different sports require different lens lengths. For example, for basketball, an 85mm lens may be sufficient for baseline action. A 400mm lens may be more suitable for soccer. Lens speed is also a critical factor. The wider the aperture, or faster the lens, the faster the shutter speed you can use.

A fast shutter speed will be able to freeze action better (see the Freezing Action section that follows). Furthermore, the wider the aperture, the more out of focus the background will be. This will reduce the distraction caused by a busy background and make the subject stand out more. Most sports photographers use a teleconverter to increase the distance of their lens. Teleconverters generally come in 1.4x or 2.0x ranges. If you use a 200mm lens with a 2.0x teleconverter, your focal length doubles. However, do bear in mind that you lose two full aperture stops. Hence, if your maximum aperture at 200mm is f/2.8, with a 2.0x teleconverter, you will only get a maximum of f/5.6. Not too bad for outdoor sports, but it could be a problem shooting low-lit indoor sports like gymnastics.

▲ A 1.4x teleconverter

▶ ▶ ▶ Camera

The next essential piece of equipment is of course the camera. Most cameras have autofocus capabilities and this helps greatly in tracking movement or fast action. However, autofocus mechanisms are not foolproof. Fortunately, many cameras and lenses have a manual focus option that can be used for more predictable sports like swimming. When using manual focus, just pre-focus on a spot where the action will happen and wait. Make sure you start releasing the shutter BEFORE the peak of the action. If you release it when you see the peak of the action, you are too late. Here is where a camera capable of shooting 8 frames per second is useful, as there is a higher chance of recording the peak of the action. With a slower camera, you'll have to depend a lot more on luck and/or skill when anticipating the peak of the action.

If you shoot a lot of portrait shots, consider getting a vertical grip with a shutter release button (if your camera does not come with one), to avoid fatigue in your arm.

▶ ▶ ▶ Camera Support

If you use a large and heavy lens such as a 300mm f/2.8, consider using a monopod to help you support your equipment. Keep one hand as close as possible to the far end of the lens to reduce camera shake. A tripod may work, but it could be more prohibitive as it does not allow movement as much as a monopod.

▶ ▶ ▶ Flash

You may also use a flash to freeze action and be more creative with panning. However, please note that some sports prohibit the use of flash as it can be distracting for the participants. If you use it, bear in mind that it may not recharge fast enough to catch up with a continuous burst of shots.

▶ A flash was used to light the subject in a dark environment. Here the flash does not distract the swimmer.

Ⓕreezing Action

Freezing action requires high shutter speeds to get crisp, sharp images. Finding the minimum shutter speed for the various sports requires experience. However, as a guide, the minimum shutter speed should be two full shutter speeds faster than the hand-hold speed. Hand-hold speed is determined by taking the reciprocal of the focal length. Say you use a 300mm lens; your hand-hold speed should be 1/300th of a second. So to freeze action, you should use a shutter speed of 1/1200. To achieve this, you may have to shoot with the aperture wide open and with a high ISO. Use a high ISO as a last resort, as it will introduce more noise into the image.

▶ A fast shutter speed was used in this case to freeze the action.

Panning

Sometimes seeing every detail may not be appealing, as you might want to indicate movement, or "give life" to the action. In this case, panning is a common technique. To do this, you follow the action with your camera, allowing the background to blur. A flash may be used in this instance to freeze the movement of the subject, providing stark contrast between it and the surrounding image. Use shutter priority and take a guess at the shutter speed needed to get the result you want. The right shutter speed is dependent on the lens, the speed of the subject, and the distance the subject is from you. Experimentation is the best way to get a feel for these factors.

◄ The photographer tracked the front cyclist and used a shutter speed fast enough to ensure that he remains sharp, but slow enough to cause the background to blur.

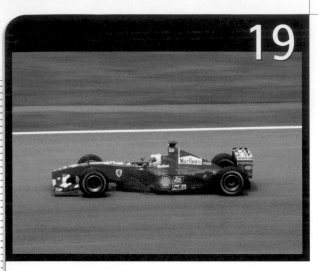

Chapter 3

19 Motorsports

Motorsports are very attractive to photographers due to the bright colors of the vehicles and fast action. In some ways, motorsports are easy to photograph, as they generally are carried out in the daytime, so fast lenses and wider apertures may not be required. Furthermore, it is easier to follow-focus the subject as the action is very predictable. However, the high speeds involved can make things challenging from time to time.

Equipment

Due to your distance from the track, you will need longer lenses to fill the frame. Shorter lenses will limit you to general wide shots of spectators and off-track shots.

To fill the frame with the subject, a minimum focal length of 200mm is ideal, but that depends a lot on where you will be situated. You may also use teleconverters to increase your focal length. If you are using a 300mm lens, consider using a monopod to help you support the lens, as hand-holding a 300mm f/2.8 lens throughout a race is a great challenge. A tripod may be used, but choose one that has a pan-tilt head to enable you to pan. Also, be aware that tripods might be more difficult to set up in a crowd.

▲ Typical results from a shorter, wide-angle lens

Location

Try to choose a suitable location to get a pleasing background. However, you are often limited due to safety concerns. If possible, do your homework before the race to get the best seats, because often you will not be able to move around during the race.

Technique

Panning can be used to show motion while keeping the subject sharp. Your pictures will not look attractive if the participants look like they are parked, so capturing the sense of motion in the scene is key. The challenge is to find the right shutter speed. Too fast, and the background will appear too sharp. Too slow and the background and the vehicles will simply look blurry. You have to balance the distance to the car, the speed of the car, and the focal length of the lens to get the best results. Use shutter priority and play around with the shutter speed to get the effect you want. Start off with shutter speeds around 1/400s. Here is where reviewing your pictures on the LCD will be useful. The good thing is the participants will pass you several times and you'll have numerous opportunities to get that perfect shot.

When panning, track the movement of the vehicle as early as possible. Spread your legs to stabilize yourself. Keep your elbows tucked into your body to stabilize your entire upper body. At the point of releasing the shutter, hold your breath to avoid camera shake, especially if your equipment is not mounted on a tripod. Try your best to follow the movement of the vehicle, and squeeze the shutter release as the vehicle approaches you. When getting the hang of panning, it's best not to have the subject too tight in the frame (to avoid cropping the front or the back of the vehicle). As you get better, you may shoot tighter shots.

▲ An example of panning with a shutter speed of 1/80s, achieving a very blurry background.　▲ A faster shutter speed of 1/125s is used here.

Instead of using the camera's autofocus, you may want to pre-focus using manual focus. Pre-focusing is commonly used by sports photographers. This is useful if your autofocus is not fast enough to track movement or if there are people walking across your field of view, causing the autofocus to focus on them instead of the action. The key to this technique is to select a background object at the location you want to release the shutter and then wait for the participants to pass. Avoid using a very large aperture; this way you'll get a bit more depth-of-field in which the subject will remain sharp.

Exposure selection is similar to other outdoor photography. Pay careful attention to uncommonly light or dark colored cars, as the in-camera exposure sensor may be fooled. As a rule of thumb, underexpose by 1/3EV to 2/3EV if you are shooting a black car, and overexpose by 1/3EV to 2/3EV when shooting a white car. This will compensate for the incorrect exposure reading of your camera. Again, check your histogram and your captured image on your LCD to make sure the subject is not over- or underexposed. Since you are shooting mainly outdoors, you can afford to use a low ISO rating like 100 to reduce digital noise in your photos.

Finally, go out and have fun while enjoying the sport. Remember, practice makes perfect, so don't get discouraged if you don't get any good shots on your first outing.

40 Digital SLR Techniques

Shooting Still-Life, Nature, and Landscape Photos

Apart from people and their activities, there are numerous other subjects suitable for photography. You will need only the most basic equipment to shoot still life. If you have macro or telephoto lenses and accessories, you'll be able to focus up-close on a variety of interesting subjects, such as insects, flowers, and birds. In Chapter 4, after discussing these possibilities, we'll go on to introduce techniques for natural, urban, and underwater landscape photography.

Chapter 4

Shooting Still Life

Some may think it boring, and it is true that it's a rather quiet indoor activity, but still-life photography challenges your mental and creative abilities to produce art out of possibly mundane objects. It requires as much thought and skill (and perhaps more) to create and express your vision through still life as it does to capture other varieties of images.

Subject Matter

One benefit, and challenge, of still life is that you have complete freedom over what to shoot. You are only limited by your imagination—whether you can see the potential in an object. Challenge yourself to find something of photographic interest in just about any object.

▲ Condensation on a refrigerated egg

- **Home/office:** Interesting pictures can be made out of tiny objects such as paper clips, nuts, bolts, and beans. Larger objects such as books and fruit can also be looked at in a different way. Forks, can openers, and alarm clocks are all fair game at home.

▲ Keys have interesting textures and shapes.

- **Flowers:** A popular subject, these are usually convenient to acquire and arrange for a series of shots.
- **Found objects:** Interesting bits of junk can be combined to create interesting compositions. Planks and cardboard can make textured backgrounds, and picked-up wire, cans, pebbles, and buttons can be worked into your scene.

▲ These circles and lines were "found" in the kitchen.

▲ Assorted hardware

- **Tabletop:** This is a genre of its own. Using ready-made items or making your own props, you can create a set very much like a miniature movie studio or a diorama, then photograph your own created world.

lighting

▶ ▶ ▶ Natural Light

Natural lighting is a good, though variable, source of light for still-life shots. To adjust the lighting, you can vary the distance of your setup from a window or door, and also diffuse the light using gauzy materials or translucent paper. If the contrast levels are too high, you could use reflectors on the other side to bounce light back into the shadows. Even a piece of paper might suffice for a small subject.

▲ A photo of a coin taken without a reflector

▲ The same photo taken using a piece of paper as a reflector

◀ Tools lit by window light

▶ ▶ ▶ Household Lamps

With the ability to set white balance, you can use any continuous light source to light your still-life setup. Table lamps and flashlights could be used, though you will probably need a tripod to keep the camera steady due to the long exposures required at low light levels. The flicker from fluorescent tubes may cause irregularities, so be cautious about using such light. Also be aware of color temperatures if different light sources are used.

▶ ▶ ▶ Electronic Flash

You may of course use direct or bounced flash to light your set. You will probably find it preferable to use the flash off-camera to avoid flat, direct lighting, so a flash cord or wireless trigger will be useful. If you don't have these, you could manually fire the flash during a long exposure (in a dark room), but trial and error (and battery drain) will be factors.

Additional Equipment

▶ ▶ ▶ Backgrounds

Besides lighting, you will find other materials handy for still-life shots. The most basic item would be a background for your subject. A large, seamless piece of paper or cloth should easily form a backdrop. Costly photographic background paper is sold in huge rolls and will only be required for large objects. You could try art or construction paper, or even a bedsheet, instead. If your room or studio is dim enough, you may not even need a background, as the far walls behind your subject may be concealed in deep shadow.

▲ No special background was needed—only the bowl was directly lit.

A light-box is another possible "background" for still-life arrangements. Objects to be photographed on a light-box are usually transparent or translucent, and are illuminated from below. Adjust your exposure, using exposure compensation or spot-metering, to allow the surface of the light-box to record as bright white.

▲ In addition to the light-box below, flash was added from the side to light the metal tips.

▶ ▶ ▶ Set Construction

You will also need to get your still-life objects into place. Tape, pins, tacks, putty, and clamps can all be put into service. Heavy objects such as phone books can be used as foundations to build on.

General Techniques

First, arrange your chosen objects in the most pleasing way possible. Whether you have one flower or twenty different pieces of junk, try out different arrangements until you find a suitable one. Vary the position and distance of the objects from the camera, and look at each object from different angles. Light the scene from different directions, whether using one or more light sources.

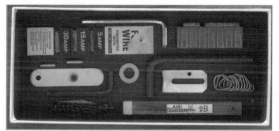

▲ Some of the contents of an old box have been arranged within it.

▲ These screws were arranged so that they appear to have fallen randomly into place.

Consider whether objects should fall entirely within the viewfinder frame, or if they can extend beyond the edges. Use DOF preview or review some test shots to gauge the effects of depth-of-field in your composition. You will most probably want to control DOF by setting the aperture in Aperture Priority or Manual mode. Arranging objects such that they are more or less equidistant from the lens will maximize the DOF. This can be done by positioning objects closer together, or by angling the camera such that the plane of focus is more aligned with the scene.

▲ Slanting this coin reduces DOF greatly, but makes for a more dynamic appearance of the embellishment.

▲ The front of the lens must be parallel with the stamp for maximum sharpness throughout the image.

Above all, consider that still-life photography is about making an image with objects, rather than making an image of objects. You should not just record a likeness of things, but communicate an idea using things.

▲ An attempt to "bring life" to tools

◀ The yellow "negative" space is as important as the pincers

Tabletop Techniques

After you have thought of the tabletop scenario you want to create, you will need to plan the construction of the set. This will depend on the lenses you have and the size of your props. If you have enough room and materials, your "tabletop" scene could well spread itself out over the floor. You might need a wider focal length to take in the whole scene. On the other hand, a tiny set might need a longer focal length or perhaps macro capability to fill the frame. With a set of a certain size, you will need a lens with suitable focal length and minimum focus distance.

▲ A "street scene" was created using a briefcase for a road surface.

The perspective of your tabletop scene will be affected by its distance from the camera. But, unlike the real world, you can create a false sense of perspective by altering the relative size of things in your scene. You can create a sense of depth, for example, by making a series of miniature trees of decreasing size; you could place them much closer to each other than if you were to use trees of the same size.

▶ The scene at f/11. The double-decker bus had to be in the back as it is slightly smaller in scale

When making props on a small scale, be aware of the thickness of your materials. When magnified, seemingly thin materials such as card stock could look too chunky. You may also need to paint the edges of materials if they are visible at your selected degree of magnification.

▶ For the final shot, a casserole dish sprayed with water was held in front of the scene to simulate a rain-spattered window.

When constructing the set, it might be useful to check the DOF occasionally. The closer the set is to the camera, the less DOF there will be. This is not necessarily a bad thing, as imperfections in your set (such as seams and paint strokes) will be thrown out of focus. On the other hand, you will need enough DOF for your scene to be recognizable!

Close-Up Photography

With a DSLR and a suitable lens, a walk in the park can become another chance for photography. Shooting flowers and insects requires patience and skill, but this form of close-up photography will reward you with a deeper appreciation of nature and its beauty.

Equipment

▶ ▶ ▶ Lenses

The basic kit you'll require includes macro equipment. The simplest form would be one or more close-up lenses, or an extension tube or two. Cheaper versions will require less outlay than a dedicated macro lens, if you are just exploring this area of photography. If you are keen on close-up shooting, however, you might just want to go straight ahead and invest in a macro lens or better-quality close-up lenses.

If you are buying a macro lens, consider getting one that gives 1:2 (half life-size) or greater magnification. You can then use a 2x teleconverter to reach life-size magnification. Also bear in mind the working distance of the lens; if you are planning to shoot timid subjects, a greater working distance lets you maintain some distance while achieving sufficient magnification.

▶ ▶ ▶ Camera Support

The next piece of equipment is a sturdy tripod. You will often need to make fine adjustments to camera position and focus, so a tripod that does not droop or wobble is virtually mandatory for critical camera placement. For subjects close to the ground, get a tripod with a reversible center column, or one that can be set up low, possibly with its center column removed.

If your tripod isn't particularly stable, you can weight it down by hanging your bag over its legs or under the center column, if there is a hook for that purpose. You can also press your hand down on the collar of the tripod neck. Avoid raising the center column high if possible, as that makes the camera less steady.

It would also be handy if you could shift your camera horizontally without moving the tripod legs. Some tripods have a center column that can be attached in horizontal position. Alternatively, some tripod heads or bellows attachments have a rack system that allows horizontal shift while maintaining camera angle. This allows you to focus at a specified magnification by moving the camera forwards and backwards, without having to refocus the lens.

▶ ▶ ▶ Other Standard Accessories

Flash is often used in close-up shooting. It provides more light in dim situations, freezes slight movement, and allows smaller apertures for greater DOF. It can also bring out colors and create highlights, in addition to filling in shadows. A flash cord or wireless control will let you use the flash off-camera. For shadowless lighting, special twin flash units or ring flashes are available; these provide even illumination.

◀ These ants are clearly visible when illuminated by flash, but the shadows cast are rather unnatural.

Many photographers find a cabled or wireless release useful for minimizing camera shake. If your remote shutter release is wired to the camera, make sure it doesn't swing about and shake the camera, especially if your tripod is not sturdy.

You may also find a mottled green or blue piece of card useful when the actual background is unsuitable and needs to be shielded. This could be a good way to simplify a composition.

Composition

Choose your background carefully. Even though close-up shots often have shallow DOF, unfocused bright spots or lines in the background can distract from your main subject. You may not always want to use shallow DOF; such shots do not tell the viewer much about the environment in which your specimen lives.

Since DOF is limited in close-up photography, you may need to compose your shots with DOF in mind. Long insects such as dragonflies and damselflies must be approached exactly side-on if you wish to render the whole body sharp from head to tail. If you want the body and wings all in sharp focus, your best bet is to shoot from directly above or below. Of course, photography is more than just fine detail, so do explore other angles.

▲ A standard head-to-tail shot

▲ This shot from above keeps just the top edge of the dragonfly focused.

▲ Going to the front gives this "mug shot."

▲ Closing in decreases DOF, but this shot concentrates on the intricate thorax and eyes while adding a more dynamic slant.

▲ Greater DOF at f/16 (left); shallow DOF at f/4 (right)

Try out different subject placements within the frame. Not every photo looks best with the subject dead center. The common "rule of thirds" is one possible guide. In horizontal format, try placing the subject to one side and (normally) facing the center of the frame. Bryan Peterson, author of the very instructive *Learning to See Creatively*, observes that positioning the subject on the right side or third of the frame somehow seems more satisfying than the left.

▲ Attention is focused on the central cluster of flowers.

▶ The eye is drawn between the two diagonally displaced clusters.

Similarly, for vertical framing, try placing the subject in the upper or lower part of the frame. Here, you may find that lower subject placement feels more "right," but be open to other possibilities.

▲ Are the flowers more pleasing on the left...   ▲ ...or on the right?

Lighting

▶ ▶ ▶ Time of Day

For the best reproduction of detail, use the lowest ISO possible. You may also want to maximize DOF with a small aperture, but watch your lighting. Though it might seem ideal, midday isn't always the best time for close-up photography because of the harsh sunlight on sunny days. A strong breeze can also be problematic. Insects may also be flying about or avoiding the heat.

Insect close-up enthusiasts recommend the early morning hours for a couple reasons: flying insects are weighed down by dew, and breezes have not begun to blow. You can always augment the low light level with flash.

For flowers, time of day may not be so crucial. Colors and contrast are generally easier to handle under soft lighting, but it is up to you to make full use of whatever lighting you have at the time.

▶ ▶ ▶ Flash

Using flash, you will need to watch your WB setting. If flash is the main light, set WB to Auto or Flash. If the flash is just for fill, you may use WB for the ambient light (e.g., shade for the bluish light of early morning).

Controlling flash output is a bit more complex when shooting small flowers or insects. Often, such subjects take up little space in the frame. The flash metering system may therefore attempt to light the background, which may result in the actual subject being overexposed.

You can use a combination of exposure compensation, flash exposure compensation, and metering modes so that the flash will not overpower your subject. Dial in exposure compensation if your background is light or dark in tone. Negative flash exposure compensation may be useful for subjects that are small or very close to the camera. If you have TTL flash metering, you can try using spot or center-weighted metering, depending on your equipment.

If your flash is off-camera, it may complicate things further. TTL control may be the best, but you can adjust settings manually. For example, you could set the flash ISO to a higher value to reduce flash output. Also, be careful if your camera uses focus distance information from the lens when metering; if the camera wrongly assumes that flash-to-subject distance is identical to camera-to-subject distance, flash output might not be correct.

General Techniques

▶ ▶ ▶ Respect for Nature

This is a very basic point, but one that is worth stating or repeating. Photographers should not harm or disturb the subjects they are shooting. On a practical level, it is necessary to treat nature with respect if we want to continue enjoying and photographing it. On another level, it would be self-contradictory to harm nature in order to celebrate its beauty.

For plants, you should at most resort to the use of string in order to gently hold back twigs that are in your way. A spray bottle of water may be used to create artificial dew.

Unlike plants, insects won't take much handling. Some photographers have been known to spray insects with a little water to prevent them from flying off. Apart from making them more vulnerable to predators, this is harmless. It is also probably the only acceptable form of interference (besides neatening up the background).

▲ Although unfocused, a dry leaf creates a light brown area behind the butterfly.

▲ Removing the leaf gives a more natural-looking background.

▶ ▶ ▶ Focusing

In standard photography, a common technique for focusing is to lock the focus using an AF point before composing the final shot. In close-up photography, however, such camera movement can subtly alter subject distance and therefore result in a slight loss of focus. Moreover, the use of teleconverters or extension tubes can cause the image to be too dim for AF to function.

Manual focus is often a better option when autofocus could be unreliable. The advantage of DSLRs is that image focus can be judged anywhere in the viewfinder frame. Roughly frame your intended picture, then manually focus till the main point of interest is sharp. You could also check the DOF preview to see what will be in focus. Fine-tune your framing after each focus adjustment, because the two are related.

▶ ▶ ▶ Subject Knowledge

If you really want to excel at nature photography, you will need to know more about your subjects. Seasonal behavior, stages of growth, likely habitats, and unique characteristics are all useful information if you wish to go beyond a cliched representation of nature. Read up or join a nature photographers' club to gain more insight.

Chapter 4

22

Photographing Birds

Birds are beautiful, and even in urban parks you can see and photograph a variety of different species. Birds are trickier to photograph than plants and insects, but the fieldcraft and photographic skill required make bird photography a rewarding challenge.

Equipment

▶ ▶ ▶ Lenses and Flash

For serious avian photographers, a 500mm or 600mm prime lens is more or less mandatory, and is sometimes coupled with a 1.4× or 2× teleconverter or extender. This can set you back thousands–if not tens of thousands–of dollars. For the more casual hobbyist, a bare minimum setup world be a 300mm prime lens with a teleconverter.

A zoom lens can theoretically be used in conjunction with a teleconverter, but this can compromise image quality when you use the longer end of the zoom, even when you stop down to a smaller aperture to improve sharpness.

In addition to your lenses, bird photography may require you to upgrade your flash because of the distances involved. To show details in dark feathers and make eyes visible, you'll want a powerful flash with zoom capability. To extend the flash range, zoom the flash head to its maximum, and consider using a flash extender (see Technique 11) to focus the beams even further.

▲ In this picture, taken with an aperture of f/8 on a 70-300mm variable-aperture zoom, the long wing feathers can be distinguished, but the rest of the plumage has turned to mush.

▲ A high-quality 80-200mm constant-aperture zoom gives better results when stopped down, but is still inferior compared to a prime lens.

▲ Flash enables a proper exposure in backlit situations.

▶ ▶ ▶ Support

With a large telephoto lens attached, a DSLR is both bulky and heavy. Such a configuration can only be handheld for brief moments, if at all. You'll want a very sturdy and stable tripod and head to support the weight. Special brackets are available for heavy lenses, allowing easy switching from landscape to portrait orientation.

Whatever you mount your equipment on, make sure that you attach it near the combined center of gravity. Usually a long telephoto will have its own tripod mounting foot to give proper balance. Do not use the tripod mount on the DSLR body.

As previously mentioned, a beanbag or a piece of clothing can stand in for a tripod if overall weight is an issue, but picture quality will be compromised somewhat.

▲ Wimberley bracket

▶ ▶ ▶ Camouflage

Some bird species are wary of human presence, so it will help to camouflage yourself a little. The simplest way is to choose drab colors for your clothes and bags. Some lenses (e.g., Canon's white L lenses) require covering up also. Custom lens covers are available, but a visit to a military surplus or supply store might turn up something at a lower price.

Some kinds of birds are so sensitive that your mere presence will cause them to abandon their nests. You don't want that on your conscience, so if you must photograph these birds you'll need to purchase or build a special shelter called a "hide" or take your photos by remote control. Going into this type of photography would require a book unto itself, but be aware that simply "taking a few photos" without proper knowledge can have disastrous consequences for your subjects.

Fieldcraft

In order to photograph birds, you must first get yourself and your equipment in proper position. Some birds may be so bold as to approach you for food, but many others will fly off as soon as you come within a certain distance of them. For the latter, good fieldcraft is needed before you can even think about using your equipment. If you know in advance what kinds of birds you're going to be photographing, it's a good idea to read up on their behavior ahead of time so you'll know how best to approach them.

▲ When accustomed to humans, some birds are quite unafraid.

▶ ▶ ▶ Movement

In addition to wearing drab clothing as previously discussed, you should move slowly as you approach your intended subjects. This applies not just to your legs, but your head and arms as well. Use deliberate movements; don't make jerky actions that can startle birds. In open parks especially, birds can spot humans well before we see them. It is not a matter of concealing our presence, but rather of avoiding behavior that will be interpreted as predatory. If you approach carefully, you might even be able to shoot from inside a vehicle.

Take your time and set up your camera and tripod slowly. You may notice that the birds are keeping an eye on you, assessing whether you pose a danger to them. If you are patient, they may eventually go back to their normal activities, and you can begin to shoot, or take a step closer to them. By waiting long enough between gradual advances, you can get closer than if you moved all at once.

▶ This changeable hawk eagle, like other raptors, required a patient and planned approach.

▶ ▶ ▶ Observation

The more you know about the behavior patterns of your subjects, the better chance you'll have of getting the shots you want. If you haven't read up beforehand, take some time to observe before you start photographing. Knowing birds' behavior allows you to recognize and shoot images that record their "true nature," as well as surprising or humorous departures from the norm.

Some birds return to specific branches or posts after each flight. If you identify these places, you can set up your shots carefully and get some nice images of the birds taking flight or alighting. Also look for places where birds sip nectar or hunt for prey; the latter can provide especially dramatic photo opportunities.

▲ If you keep your lens trained on a popular perch, you will probably get numberous photo opportunities.

◀ Both the skill and beauty of this blue-throated bee-eater are captured in this image.

▲ The neck of this heron is poised to deliver a lightning strike.

▲ The heron with its eel catch.

Photographing Birds in Flight

If you want to get good shots of birds in flight, you'll need to pay special attention to freezing motion and to exposure.

▶ ▶ ▶ Freezing Motion

You'll need a fast shutter speed to freeze the motion of flying birds. If they are moving quickly and unpredictably, you'll need an even higher shutter speed to allow you to shoot handheld. Alternatively, you can try panning with slower shutter speeds.

▲ This shot captures the little tern just as it hits the water.

You can usually keep moving subjects in focus with continuous AF. It helps greatly if your lens has ultrasonic focusing. If AF cannot lock on or keep up, you'll have to focus manually. Set focus to a specific distance, and release the shutter just as (or just before) the bird comes into focus.

You'll also need to choose a suitable drive mode. Continuous drive at more than 2 frames per second (fps) is enough to record an action sequence but at least 4 or 5 fps would be better. Too slow a frame rate can actually make it more difficult to capture the perfect moment. You might do better learning to anticipate and capture a single shot at just the right instant.

▲ Shooting in continuous drive mode can help you capture a variety of wing positions.

▶ ▶ ▶ Exposure

If you're shooting birds against a background of sky, your exposure setting must take the brightness of the sky into consideration to avoid underexposing the subject.

If evaluative or matrix metering results in underexposure, use center-weighted, partial, or spot metering instead. This way, you can restrict the metering to exclude most of the sky and take a reading mostly from the subject.

Whichever metering pattern you use, you may need to dial in exposure compensation. This depends on how precisely the metering pattern isolates the bird from the background, and what tonal range the plumage is. Generally, bright sky and light colors require extra exposure, while dark tones require negative compensation.

▲ Red-Wattled Lapwing shot using positive exposure compensation

Composition

Good photos are more than just properly exposed shots; the right composition is crucial. You want the right relationship between your subject (or subjects) and the immediate environment, as well as the more distant background.

▶ ▶ ▶ Background

With long telephoto lenses, the DOF is usually limited. Objects in the background will be unfocused, but color and brightness remain possible distractions. Try to position yourself so that the background complements your subject.

▲ The defocused white spot to the left of the munia is a little distracting.

▲ This shot is slightly different, but more satisfactory.

It is traditional in nature photography to avoid anything manmade in the background, but you are free to ignore this rule if you choose.

▶ A humorous look at a particular urban park "habitat."

▶ ▶ ▶ Depth-of-Field

A shallow DOF will make your subject stand out from a distant background easily. Use the DOF preview or image review to gauge the effect of your aperture setting, especially if you want enough DOF to make the whole bird sharp.

▲ The DOF and bokeh of a picture should not distract from the main subject.

▲ A narrow DOF picks out a Malayan plover from the sandy ground, while retaining some sense of its environment.

On the other hand, you may want to use more DOF in order to show some of the bird's natural environment. One technique is to position yourself so that both the bird and some relevant feature (such as a branch) are the same distance from your lens. That way, both can be in focus at the same time. Alternatively, you can simply set the aperture to provide enough DOF for the whole scene.

▶ ▶ ▶ Framing

You'll probably want to put your subject in the middle of the frame while focusing, but the final picture may not always look the best if the subject is dead center. Images often look more balanced if the bird is to one side, facing the center of the frame.

▶ Leave space in front for the bird to look into.

As always, try vertical and horizontal formats to see which is most effective. You could even try tilting the camera.

Where appropriate, zoom in on details or parts of the bird's body. This way, you will be able to focus on expressions and unique or beautiful features.

▲ Try framing a different way for greater impact.

▶ Bird portraits need not always show the whole body.

▶ ▶ ▶ Lighting

Make the best use of the natural light available. If the sun is shining strongly, try to shoot on the sunlit side for the best colors and contrast. Watch out for harsh shadows being cast.

▲ Diffuse light on a rainy day can also be good for some shots.

▲ Strong lighting creates rich colors.

You can also take good pictures in gloomier weather, though your shutter speed may need to be slower. When there is cloud cover, the sky becomes a huge softbox, enveloping everything in an even, perhaps shadowless light.

▶ ▶ ▶ Catchlights

Last but not least, "catchlights"–reflections in the eyes caused by a bright light source–are an important part of bird photography. They add sparkle and life to a bird portrait. Some photographers use flash to add a catchlight, even when there is enough light for an exposure without flash.

▲ Natural light creates a beautiful catchlight in this sidelit shot.

▲ A fine shot, but the eye lacks a catchlight.

▲ Flash adds catchlight, making a subtle difference.

Successful bird photography requires lots of patience, practice, and experience, so get out and about, and start shooting!

23 Panoramas

Computer "stitching" gives new meaning to the concept of wide-angle landscape photography. With a tripod and just about any lens, you can produce seamless panoramic views using your DSLR and software. This section outlines the simple procedure for creating panoramic landscapes.

Equipment

The individual shots that form a panorama are easiest to join up when they can be perfectly aligned. Thus, while a tripod is not absolutely essential, it does make for less work. Use a tripod that allows for movement in just one direction at a time. A ballhead, while preferred by many for the previous two techniques, may not be useful here if it does not have a separate panning movement.

Preferably, use a lens with minimal distortion, since exaggerated or curved perspective at the frame edges might not align well with the next frame.

You may not be able to use a polarizing filter since the camera angle will change with every shot, and with it the polarizing effect.

Composition

The first step is to plan your panoramic scene. For simple horizontal panoramas, the resulting image will be equal to or less than the height of one DSLR image. Note that you can use the camera in either wide or tall format. Similar guidelines apply for vertical panoramas. Either way, including some nearer objects can give a better impression of depth than a scene with elements all at the same distance.

Other than simple linear panoramas, you can also take "joiner" pictures. Instead of a single row of images, joiner pictures are more like a patchwork or quilt of images. You will need to move your camera in more than one dimension to capture your chosen scene frame by frame. You can do it methodically with careful tripod adjustment, or simply with a handheld technique for a more roughly fitted look.

Be cautious when shooting in changing conditions. Changing light levels or color temperature are more likely in the early or late hours of the day, while movement due to wind and waves can affect just about any scene. When adjacent shots vary significantly, they will be harder to merge seamlessly. If you want to take panoramic sunsets, for example, you should finalize your settings, then make your series of shots as quickly as possible.

Technique

First, check your view by looking through the viewfinder while rotating the camera on the tripod. Assess whether the camera is level (assuming you want it that way), and whether the overall composition is free from unwanted elements.

Decide where you will start and end your panoramic series, and how many frames you will need. You must leave a sizeable amount of overlap between adjacent frames so that computer stitching will be more successful. Also, try to put important elements in the middle of a frame and not split them between frames. Viewers will be more likely to scrutinize these parts of a photo, so put the "seams" of your panorama elsewhere.

To maintain consistency between the individual shots, you should use the same focus distance, DOF, exposure, and WB. It will probably be easiest to use manual focus as well as the manual (M) exposure mode for panoramas. Set both the focus and aperture, taking into account the nearest and farthest parts of your entire scene. Meter for the most important part of your scene, and set the shutter speed accordingly. For WB, use a fixed value, or set custom WB using a suitable reference.

Now, all you need to do is shoot your planned series of shots, beginning at your identified starting point. Be careful not to jar the camera and tripod while shifting the camera, and move the equipment smoothly.

Computer Stitching

Many standalone programs for stitching panoramas are available. In addition, graphics editing suites often have image stitching capability. The better ones adjust for curved perspective, in addition to blending images seamlessly. Here, Canon's PhotoStitch utility will be used for demonstration.

Before running the stitching program, view your images side-by-side on screen to check if the brightness and color match sufficiently. If not, you may need to edit them before you begin stitching.

▲ Import the images for stitching and check that they are arranged in the right order.

▲ Set the value for lens focal length, if perspective correction is available.

▲ Activate the stitching. The computer will attempt to join the images automatically.

▲ You can manually adjust the overlap between two images.

▲ Check the seams to see whether they are smoothly joined. Check also that the horizon and other important lines are naturally rendered.

▲ After it has been completed, enlarge the panorama image.

▲ Drag one image over the other so that they overlap as neatly as possible.

▲ Finally, you have the option of cropping the panorama to a neat rectangle, or leaving it with its rough edges.

▲ Canon PhotoStitch has a Wide Display Option; in this case, it gives a straighter horizon line.

▲ The final image is stitched together from 13 separate images.

24

Night Scenes

Parks and the great outdoors are not the only places you can take great pictures. The city can be an object of photographic exploration just as it has been an object of literary imagination. Shooting at night can add additional "drama" to urban shots. In this technique, we'll show you the ropes.

Location

Basically, you have to know the appearance of a place by night. When natural ambient light is traded for artificial lighting, scenes may be transformed from their daytime selves. If you are familiar with the location, look at the scene from different viewpoints to discover interesting compositions.

If you're interested in sunsets or sunrises, take time to note their corresponding locations relative to the scene. Sometimes, the sun lights up clouds in other parts of the sky, and this can create a wonderful effect.
Just make sure you're in position in time to catch the light.

▲ Shooting before the sky has totally darkened will preserve some color.

Reflections in glass or water (whether puddles or the sea) are often a useful element in night scenes. Light streaks from traffic (achieved through the use of slow shutter speeds) are another way to augment picture composition. Visualize the light streaks as lines in your composition.

▶ The lights from traffic underscore the overall composition.

Settings

● **ISO:** For the smoothest images, use the lowest ISO setting. Higher ISOs may introduce noise and degrade fine detail. You may, however, try shooting at high ISOs if you happen not to have a tripod. This applies to general scenes as well as those involving fireworks.

▲ This scene could be shot handheld at about 1/15s using ISO 800.

● **Contrast:** Although urban night scenes are generally dark, they often contain bright, spot sources of light, such as street lamps. The overall contrast of the scene can be quite high as a result. You could attempt to control this by using a low contrast setting, especially to hold detail in the lighter areas. Most of the images in this section were taken using a low-contrast parameter.

● **Shutter speed and aperture:** With the low light levels at night, long exposures become the norm. Choose a shutter speed and aperture combination depending on how much subject movement you want to record (if any), and how much DOF you require.

▲ With an approximate exposure of 1/3s at f/4, you get a more accurate impression of the water surface.

▲ An exposure of 5s at f/16 makes the sea look very smooth and calm. Neither is more correct; these are merely two ways of interpreting the same scene.

▲ A one-second exposure gives a hint of the many people strolling along the cafes and bars.

▲ A ten-second exposure clears the view, but makes the scene look more deserted.

● **White balance:** When photographing night scenes, it isn't always necessary or even desirable to neutralize the main color cast, especially since viewers will normally understand that artificial lighting is involved, and may appreciate a bit of color in an otherwise dark scene. Auto or Sunny WB presets are possible starting points, but there are really few firm rules here.

▲ Auto WB gives a neutral result, but is much bluer that what is actually perceived.

▲ Daylight WB is a bit too yellow; the actual color temperature should have been somewhere in-between.

● **Noise reduction:** For long exposures of several seconds or longer, you could try using your DSLR's in-camera noise reduction. This might increase image-processing time significantly, however. Alternatively, you could use noise reduction software on your computer (see Chapter 6).

▲ 100% crop without noise reduction

▲ With noise reduction; this 100% crop does not show much improvement.

▲ The full image (without noise reduction)

Handling

Besides using a tripod and being very gentle with the shutter release, there are no major difficulties where handling is concerned.

● **Exposure:** You could let the camera suggest the exposure using evaluative (matrix) metering, or be more precise using spot or partial metering on an area of tone. Avoid letting light shine into the viewfinder from behind the camera. This light may affect the meter reading.

The review image may not be a good guide for adjusting the exposure. Instead, use the histogram when reviewing images. Many night scenes, having rather dark backgrounds and spots of bright light, will have a U-shaped histogram, representing the abundance of dark and light pixels. If there are areas in your picture that should have shadow detail (i.e., they are not totally black), check that there is information in the left quarter or third of the histogram, and not just at the extreme left edge.

● **Focus:** If it is too dark to use autofocus, switch to manual focus. If your lens has a distance scale, you could use this to help, especially when stopping down to a smaller aperture for greater DOF.

● **Shutter release:** If you are not able to keep the camera steady while pressing the shutter release, you could use a cabled or wireless remote release. Alternatively, you could use the camera's self-timer and set it to fire five or ten seconds after you press the button. It might be useful to remember that being too near traffic could result in ground vibrations from vehicles passing by.

● **Zooming/panning:** This last handling technique takes practice to perfect, and can be clichéd if overused. First, set your exposure and note the shutter speed. With your eye at the viewfinder (and the shutter open), move the camera and/or the lens zoom ring, paying special attention to the brightest points in the frame. You can vary the speed of movement; the slower the movement, the brighter that part will turn out. Adjust the tightness of the tripod head so that it gives some support without hindering your desired camera movement. Practice completing your panning or zooming movement within the time limit. You can get some really interesting shots using this method.

Alternatively, you could use the Bulb exposure mode, and cover the lens with a black card when you want to shut out light. This way, you can even create a "multiple exposure" effect, with or without zooming or panning. This also applies to shots of fireworks or lightning.

25

Underwater

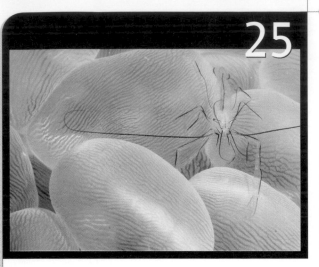

If you are fortunate enough to be a diver as well as a photographer, underwater photography will enable you to combine and enhance both activities. From tiny fish and seahorses to huge rays and corals, truly amazing sights lie beneath the surface, and your DSLR can help you bring some of these treasures back to dry land.

Equipment

Even more than bird photography, underwater photography requires specialized equipment that may call for a significant investment.

▶ ▶ ▶ Underwater Housings

The core of an underwater setup is protective underwater housing made specifically for your DSLR model. Some manufacturers of housings are Aquatica, Ikelite, and Sea & Sea. Before you make a purchase, confirm that the housing has knobs and buttons on the outside that correspond to the controls on your camera–so that you can access the settings while underwater. The more crucial controls are those for metering mode, exposure compensation, flash exposure compensation (if you're using TTL strobes), shutter speed and/or aperture, and switching from manual focus to autofocus.

You will also need lens ports compatible with both the underwater housing and the lenses that you plan on using. Such ports should have outer controls for manual focus or zoom ring operation, as appropriate. Flat-front ports are used for macro and close-up shooting, while dome ports are used for wide-angle lenses. Lens port extensions are available to allow teleconverters and close-up diopters to be attached.

If you don't want to spend the money for a rigid housing, you could try a flexible plastic housing such as those made by Ewa-Marine. Most buttons should be operable through the clear plastic, but flexible housings are generally not rated for greater depths and have limited compatibility with lenses and accessories. Some flexible housings allow you to use a topside (non-aquatic) flash unit—also a cost-cutting option—but you will not be able to use underwater flash units for optimum image quality.

▶ ▶ ▶ Flash Strobes

Underwater strobes provide flash illumination, which is a necessity in many underwater situations. To avoid dark corners in your photos, make sure that the strobe light's angle of coverage matches or exceeds your lens' field of view. TTL compatibility with your DSLR will be a great advantage. You can use either one strobe, or two for better coverage of your subject. Some strobes can be used in slave mode, which is useful when you want flash from off-camera; your dive buddy could help hold and aim a slave strobe, for example.

Strobes are attached to the housing with adjustable arms, and to the camera with sync cords. It is best to have a clear idea about the lighting effects you wish to achieve before you buy strobes and accessories, as there are various designs and configurations available.

▶ ▶ ▶ Lenses

Due to the color-absorbing properties of water at greater distances, most underwater photographers use wide-angle or fisheye lenses, and shoot as close as possible to the subject. You can keep your standard zoom fixed at the widest setting, or purchase a wide-angle prime or zoom lens if that isn't wide enough. You need to check whether the lens can focus properly when used with a dome port, as the curved port front creates a closer virtual image, and your focus should be on that, rather than the actual subject distance. If the minimum focus distance is not small enough, you can decrease it by adding a close-up lens.

For close-up and macro shots, the cheaper options are to add close-up lenses, extension tubes, or a teleconverter. You can use them in combination as well. Note, though, that the added length might require lens port extensions, which may be costly; check the overall measurements carefully. Tubes and teleconverters also reduce the already limited light coming through the lens. If you have the budget, or already own one, a macro lens is ideal, since it does not compromise light and image quality.

▶ ▶ ▶ Care and Maintenance

Familiarize yourself thoroughly with your equipment before venturing near the water. Learn to operate all the controls on your housing and how to adjust strobe positioning before you dive, so you won't waste precious dive time figuring things out.

Inspect all the O-ring seals and make sure there are no fine particles on them, or anything that could cause seepage under pressure. It is a good idea to do a test by submerging the empty housing to check for leaks.

After use, rinse the housing and strobes well in fresh water before opening the seals. Make sure you are in a dry area away from sea spray when you open the housing. After your trip, follow your equipment manufacturer's instructions regarding maintenance and cleaning before storing the underwater kit away.

General Techniques

▶ ▶ ▶ Lighting

One important thing to keep in mind is the color-absorbing nature of water. Whether sunlight or strobe light, water transmits and absorbs wavelengths and colors at different rates. After around 3 meters, reds are absorbed. Subsequently, orange, yellow, and then green disappear. Finally, after the light has traveled through about 20 meters of water, only blues and purples are left.

▶ This shot is almost monochromatic, but still captures a sense of rhythm.

As a result, the ability to adjust WB with DSLRs is of limited use, as the colors cannot be balanced when they are simply not there. But you can use WB settings to lessen excessive blue in shallow waters, or even accentuate the blues seen at greater depths.

In deeper waters, you'll need to provide light much closer to the subject using strobes if you want to record your chosen subject in a full spectrum of colors.

Get as close as you can to your main subject; more water in-between means more colors lost. Also, place your strobes as close as is practical, keep in mind that the light has to travel from the strobe to the subject, then from the subject to the lens.

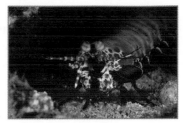

▲ Flash restores true colors.

▶ ▶ ▶ Balanced Fill-Flash

When using flash for wide-angle underwater scenes, you will probably want to capture the brilliant blue in the background. Set your exposure to match the background illumination, then use flash (preferably in TTL mode) to achieve proper exposure for the foreground. You could use Manual (M) mode to select the shutter speed and aperture, or Shutter Priority (S/Tv) mode to let the camera set the aperture. In both cases, you need to watch the exposure readout in the viewfinder to set an appropriate shutter speed or aperture.

Alternatively, you could try using slow-sync flash mode, though you have to watch out for shutter speeds that are too slow.

▲ Flash balanced with ambient exposure captures a blue background that resembles sky.

If flash makes the foreground too bright, you can use flash exposure compensation to reduce strobe output. Try using a value of −1 for a start. If the highlights tend to be overexposed, you may also want to try setting the contrast/tone processing parameter to low. You can adjust the tonal balance later on your computer.

If you want to adjust strobe output manually, you will need to know the underwater guide number of your strobes for the ISO you will be using, in either metric or imperial units. The following formulas apply:

$$\frac{\text{Guide Number}}{\text{distance}} = \text{aperture(f-number)}$$

$$\frac{\text{Guide Number}}{\text{aperture(f-number)}} = \text{distance}$$

▶ ▶ ▶ Backscatter

Water contains small particles that can show up as white speckles if illuminated by flash, interfering with your image. This undesirable effect is known as "backscatter," and the best way to prevent it is to avoid lighting the water in front of the subject with your strobes. Position the strobes away from the camera and lens, and aim them such that the light catches your subject but not the water in front of it.

Since strobes emit a cone of light rather than a narrow beam, position the strobe heads to light the subject using the edge of the light, rather than the center. If you aim the strobe dead center at the subject, the wider angle of coverage may light the water in front and cause backscatter.

▲ A small amount of backscatter was unavoidable due to the restricted angle and the environment.

Placing a strobe to the side decreases backscatter, but creates shadows on the opposite side of the subject. This is one reason some photographers opt to use two strobes, one on each side. These strobes may be used at different power, though, to create a more three-dimensional effect. One is used as the main light, the other as fill-in.

To help minimize backscatter, be careful not to stir up particles or cause bubbles with your hands or fins.

▶ ▶ ▶ Fieldcraft

Like other kinds of wildlife, marine creatures need time to get comfortable with your proximity, and are best approached slowly and gradually.

It will help if you learn as much as you can about underwater life. Knowing the right tides and times, as well as habitats and methods of camouflage, will increase the likelihood of seeing less-common creatures and events.

Above all, have respect for flora and fauna, and for reefs. Do not damage or remove anything swimming or still, as the ecosystem is a sensitive one. Furthermore, your shots will not be authentic if you have to manipulate the scene to get them.

▲ This shot of a striped fang blenny required a careful approach.

▲ Sperm exchange between Nembrotha lineolata sea slugs

Subjects

▶ ▶ ▶ Underwater Life

The sea offers a wide variety of possible subjects for photography: underwater creatures, seascapes, and even other divers.

The underwater environment is teeming with life. If you stop and take the time to inspect a small area for signs of life, you can find many tiny creatures. Some camouflaged organisms will take a little while to spot.

▶ Left: This arrowhead crab is picked out from the background using flash.

▶ ▶ Right: This flathead crocodile fish is nearly invisible beneath the sand.

You could also take macro shots of details of larger animals, to create abstract images of their amazing colors and patterns.

At close-up distances, DOF is severely limited. You should therefore choose a suitable aperture to keep the necessary parts of the scene in focus. Also, position the lens perpendicular to the desired plane of focus, so that the DOF covers the important points.

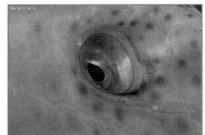

▲ The eye of a filefish

▶ Shooting slightly from the side helps to keep both fish in focus.

High magnifications increase the effect of any camera shake. Therefore, use a shutter speed high enough to freeze any camera or subject movement. Often, this results in the background going black from underexposure.

Lighting is generally added from the front. However, translucent objects may be lit from the side or back to show their delicate structures.

▲ The translucent nature of the shrimp and bubble coral is brought out better by aiming a strobe from the back.

▶ This peacock anemone could also be lit from the rear or side for a different look.

▶ ▶ ▶ Seascapes

When shooting underwater landscapes (or seascapes), remember the standard landscape axiom that the foreground should contain something of interest. Go close to the foreground creatures or reef structures, and light them with strobes if necessary, balancing the exposure for the background.

Frame the scene so that the objects are positioned to create visual "flow," and remember that off-center subject placement may give better balance.

Sometimes you can shoot without strobes. Shooting upwards to capture silhouettes of divers or schooling fish, or downwards to photograph wrecks—these are times when a blue scene may be acceptable and even desirable. If the sun's image is present in the frame, you can use spot or partial metering to gauge exposure using the midtones in the scene.

◄ ◄ Left: Positioning the foreground to the side creates symmetry with the slopes in the background.

◄ Right: Shooting upwards with only ambient light creates an ethereal mood.

▶ ▶ ▶ Divers

If you plan to shoot underwater portraits of your friends, or use other divers to add human interest or scale to your images, it is best to discuss it before the dive so that everyone knows what is expected.

For portraits, be careful to position your lighting to avoid shadows or reflections caused by masks. As far as possible, make sure the eyes are in focus and well lit. In action shots, if the subject's eyes are visible, make sure they are looking at the focus of the action and not at the camera.

▲ It is preferable to shoot when there are no distracting bubbles.

40 Digital SLR Techniques

Storing and Sharing Your Images

When you return from a trip, whether it was half a day or a month long, the next exciting step is to transfer your images to your computer so you can share them with friends and family.

In this chapter, you'll learn techniques for organizing your images. We'll also cover methods for sharing them—either on screen or through physical prints.

Chapter 5

26
Transferring Pictures from the Camera

Transferring files from your camera to your computer is obviously a critical part of the DSLR experience. Your computer, in addition to storing your images, allows you to organize and edit photos with great efficiency and freedom.

Connection to Computer

You basically have two choices when transferring the contents of your memory card to the computer. You can connect your camera, with the card in it, directly to the computer, or you can put the card in a card reader connected to the computer. In any case, you should use the fastest transfer rate available.

- **FireWire/IEEE 1394:** This connection supports the highest transfer speeds, but you must have compatible hardware. Not all computers or DSLRs have FireWire capability.

- **USB 2.0 High Speed:** This is the next option, relatively more common, and available on most newer computers, card readers, and cameras. Note that both the computer and camera/reader must be high-speed in order to get the faster transfer rate. Otherwise transfer only takes place at the slower rate.

- **USB 2.0 Full Speed:** Transferring at a more sluggish speed, this option is suitable when time and transfer speed aren't critical.

- **USB 1.1:** Data takes the longest to travel along this type of interface. If either end of your transfer process (either the computer or camera/reader) is using USB 1.1, data transfer will seem to take ages. The large file sizes produced by DSLRs generally mean that this older technology is too slow for comfort.

Since all USB devices use the same ports, you will need to check the documentation for your hardware to verify the USB speed available to you.

It is recommended that you use a FireWire or USB 2.0 High Speed connection so that you can move to the next step as soon as possible.

Mass Storage Mode

In mass storage mode, the memory card will be treated like a disk drive by the computer. In Windows, a drive letter will be assigned to the memory card. On a Mac, the card will appear as a disk drive. Card readers will always operate as mass storage. You may be able to use your DSLR in mass storage mode.

When you connect the memory card to Windows in this mode, an option box may pop up, giving you a selection of programs you can use to view the contents of the card. Windows Explorer is usually a quick and convenient option, allowing you to browse the contents of the card like you would a file folder.

PTP Mode

This stands for Picture Transfer Protocol. When you connect your DSLR in PTP mode, it will be recognized by Windows as a device (like a printer). You will see a different pop-up option box. Only programs that work with digital cameras (in PTP mode) may be used to view, transfer, or print images directly from the card in the camera.

Organizing in Folders

Digital photos can proliferate at an alarming rate. When you download your images from your camera, it is best to store them in folders straightaway. You can easily use Windows Explorer to create folders to sort your pictures by date, event, or location.

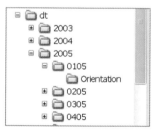

You could also create duplicates of your photos for editing or resizing and place them in a working folder. The originals would be stored in an archival folder so that they do not get accidentally altered or deleted. This way, if you make a mistake, you can start all over again with the original image file.

27

Using an Image Browser

You will need to see your photos on screen in order to edit and organize your collection. For basic work, Windows Explorer will do, but dedicated image browsers will make tasks easier once your collection grows and things get more complicated.

Basic Tasks

Simple forms of organization can be handled directly in Windows or through a separate program.

▶▶▶ Organizing Images
Whichever method you use, it is often useful to view images as thumbnails. This works like a traditional contact sheet, allowing you to quickly group files according to subject matter.

▶▶▶ Pruning and Deleting
The next step is to examine images in detail. Unsatisfactory shots, as well as unneeded duplicates, can be deleted. This is not just to save space on your hard disk; it can waste a lot of your time to look through hundreds or thousands of images. Unnecessary files are not worth keeping, and spending a bit of time at this stage will save you time later.

For this stage in the organizational process, you will need to magnify your photos to different degrees. To begin, sizing each image to fit the whole screen enables you to check the overall exposure and composition. This is a good way to tell immediately which photos are good and which ones aren't.

To check for further detail and sharpness, you'll want to view each image at 100%. Using this view, each pixel of your image is displayed by one pixel on the screen—so you're seeing all the image data in your photo. You will only be able to see a small part of the image at any given time, but you can scroll around to check the important parts of your photo. In this way, you can review the finer details to make sure everything is optimal.

Remember, if you decreased the sharpening parameter on your DSLR, the image may not appear sharp at this stage, even though it was taken with proper focus. Use an image-editing program to improve the sharpness of the final image.

Tagging Files

To make it easier to find files, some programs allow you to tag photos using visual symbols or words. These tags make it possible to locate images by searching for specific tags. You will need an image browser to do this.

Adobe Photoshop Album Starter Edition (http://www.adobe.com) allows you to create tags that appear as symbols beside the tagged photos. You can also enter a caption and notes.

With Picasa (http://picasa.google.com/index.html), you may tag a photo with a star; you can also use keywords to describe a photo.

Think carefully before choosing words to associate with your photos. Use words that are obvious and natural to you. Avoid using more than one word for each concept. For example, you could label your trip photos with either "holiday" or "vacation," but if you use both, or can't remember which one you chose for any given photo, you could have difficulty locating the right pictures in the future. Spelling and punctuation are also important. "New York" could be labeled "NY," "N.Y.," or "newyork." It pays to be consistent with your naming system.

Additional Capabilities

With your photos organized using folders and tags, you are ready to go on to image editing and manipulation. But many image browsers offer more features which can be useful to you; make sure you've exhausted the potential of your software before moving on.

▶ ▶ ▶ Quick Fixing

If you just need to print snapshots or convert your images for Web publishing, some programs offer various user-friendly editing and conversion options. Picasa even allows you to view histogram information during editing.

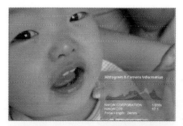

Picasa also has menus for easy application of special effects; these are often faster and easier to use than their counterparts in fully functional editing programs.

Adobe Photoshop Album Starter Edition has a useful viewing mode that shows before-and-after versions of the image side-by-side for easy comparison. This allows you to apply basic effects knowing exactly what you'll end up with.

Both programs do not overwrite the original files when you edit, so you do not have to worry that your original files will be degraded by the streamlined editing.

▶ ▶ ▶ RAW Image Viewing

Some programs, including IrfanView (http://www.irfanview .com), enable you to view and edit RAW files. The quality of the output will not be as good as dedicated RAW converters, but these programs do give basic functionality in a convenient package.

▶ ▶ ▶ EXIF Data

Each DSLR image contains EXIF (Exchangeable Image File Format) metadata that records the camera settings used for that image. Values such as shutter speed, aperture, ISO, and WB settings are all recorded as part of the image. Some programs allow you to read this data, providing you with a very detailed record of your camera settings for each shot. Although third-party programs exist, those made by camera manufacturers are the most reliable. Canon's ZoomBrowser EX reads EXIF data from Canon digital cameras.

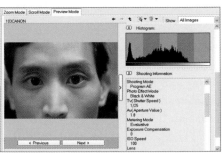

▶ ▶ ▶ Batch Renaming

This is an extremely useful function. Rather than having generic file names (or numbers), you can give files a more specific prefix that places groups of files within context. Programs such as IrfanView allow you to rename a batch of photos easily, using the original serial numbers or starting a new series entirely. This way, you run less risk of having files with duplicate names. You will also be able to locate pictures based on their file names.

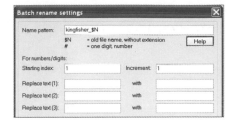

Software Options

▶ ▶ ▶ Freeware

There are quite a few free image browser programs. Adobe Photoshop Album Starter Edition, IrfanView, and Picasa are some of the well-known ones already mentioned. They are surprisingly full-featured given that they are free.

Camera manufacturers also provide software with their DSLRs. Canon's Digital Photo Professional and ZoomBrowser EX, and Nikon's Picture Project and Nikon View, are some examples. Their main attractions are RAW image processing using the manufacturer's algorithms, and more detailed EXIF information.

▶ ▶ ▶ Commercial Image Browsers

You can purchase programs such as ACDSee (http://www.acdsystems.com), Adobe Photoshop Album (http://www.adobe.com), BreezeBrowser Pro (http://www.breezesys.com), and Paint Shop Photo Album (http://www.corel.com). These programs may offer extra functionality; you should do a comparison with the free programs to see if you really need to buy an image browser.

If you already have a full-fledged image editing program, such as Adobe Photoshop, Corel Paint Shop Pro, or Ulead PhotoImpact (http://ulead.com), you will probably not need a separate image browser. These programs come with their own image browsers which are designed to work seamlessly with the editing program.

28

Chapter 5

Storage Considerations

One advantage of digital images over film is that they may be stored and reproduced without suffering any degradation in quality. In reality, however, computer files are susceptible to errors and viruses, and storage media does degrade over time. We thus need to give some thought to the storage of our digital photos. In addition to your computer's hard disk, you should seriously consider at least one backup option.

Additional Hard Disks

You could use another hard disk to back up your data. This disk could be installed within the same computer, providing convenient access when you want to back up more files or retrieve old ones. Alternatively, the hard disk could be placed in its own casing and connected to your computer via USB or FireWire. Your data can then be stored in another location, providing an added level of security.

Using a hard disk may be seen as putting all your eggs in one basket. A hard disk may be vulnerable to data loss over time, or it may even crash, corrupting valuable data. You might even lose all the data on the disk. Hard disks may last for several years, but the actual life span is not predictable. If you use hard disks, you should transfer the files to a new hard disk every 2 to 5 years.

▲ Iomega external hard disk

CD-R Discs

Being cheap, light, and easy to store, these are a popular way to store data. An average CD-R can store about 700 megabytes (MB) of data (about 650 MB after formatting). You will need to install a CD burner to record, or "burn," data to CD-R discs.

▲ Verbatim CD-R

Be careful not to get fingerprints or scratches on the disc, both before and after burning data to it, as they can affect the writing or reading of your data. It's a good habit to always hold discs by their edges. Use a soft-tipped marker or adhesive labels specially made for CD-Rs, because other inks or gums may damage the dye layer on which the data is burned.

CD-Rs can be written to only once, but you can usually add data in subsequent burn "sessions" until the disc is full. To do this, you have to set the CD burning software so that it does not finalize the disc. If the disc is finalized before it is full, the rest of the blank space will no longer be usable. CD-RWs are a rewritable disc format, so they may be erased and recorded with new data. However, their estimated life span is less than that of CD-Rs, so they should not be used for long-term archiving.

Even CD-Rs may not last a lifetime; poor quality discs may record successfully, only to fail after a year's storage. Generally, life expectancy can range from several years to several decades. To archive your valuable photos, it is worth spending more money on high-quality media. Store the discs in a cool, dark environment with low humidity (similar conditions for photographic equipment, conveniently enough). Wipe off any fingerprints or dirt gently, in straight lines from the center to the edges, using a lint-free cloth. You could also use lens-cleaning tissue or a microfiber cloth.

DVD Discs

Using newer technology, a standard DVD is capable of storing 4.7 gigabytes (GB) of data (about 4.3 GB after formatting); a double-layered DVD, 8.5 GB. These are handy capacities, given that the high-resolution photos produced by DSLRs can take up to several megabytes each. While blank recordable DVD discs cost more than CD-Rs, the price per megabyte is actually lower. If you have a DVD disc burner, this option is better than CD-Rs.

You can use DVD-R or DVD+R discs, depending on which type is compatible with your DVD burner. DVD+RW and DVD-RW discs are rewritable, but are not recommended for the same reasons as CD-RWs. Discs and DVD burning drives both come in a range of write and read speeds; be aware that higher speeds cost more.

DVD discs should be handled and stored with the same care as CD-Rs. If you buy quality DVDs, they should have a life span similar to that of good CD-Rs.

▲ Imation DVD+R.

Standalone Disc Burners

If you do not have access to a computer, or do not wish to use one, a standalone disc burner allows you to plug in your memory card or camera (via USB), and transfer the images directly to a CD or DVD. Examples are the Delkin BurnAway, the Apacer Disc Steno, and the Sony Photo Vault. Look for one that allows you to verify the files after copying, before you delete the original images or reformat your memory card! A battery-operated model will allow you to transfer images anywhere.

29

Online Photo Albums

After you have organized and backed up your photos, you may want to share them with others. The Internet allows you to share your photos with family and friends virtually anywhere they can get connected to the Web. Some Web sites offer online albums to make the task much simpler.

Resizing Photos

DSLRs produce high-resolution digital photos, suitable for printing at high output resolution. For online sharing, however, you need to consider the screen size and display resolution of computer monitors.

▶ ▶ ▶ Display Resolution

The display resolutions for monitors follow standard horizontal and vertical pixel measurements. At the lower end, a few older systems may still be at 640 × 480, while some larger monitors can display 1600 × 1200 pixels on their screens. New wide-screen formats do not follow the 4:3 aspect ratio, and this can make things even more complicated. But it is safe to assume a standard 800 × 600 or 1024 × 768 display resolution when resizing your images for the Web. Your images have to be smaller than that to leave space for margins and menu bars, however.

Using your image browser or editing program, you can do batch resizing for selected photos; this allows you to modify groups, or "batches," of photos automatically. Some programs ask you to specify the maximum dimensions you wish to resize to. For photos to be viewed large on screen, you can resize to a maximum of 640 or 800 pixels width, or a maximum of 480 or 600 height. Other programs may ask you to specify the percentage of size reduction you wish to apply. For example, if your DSLR image dimensions are 3000 × 2000, resizing to 20% will result in a smaller image measuring 600 × 400 pixels.

For thumbnails on a Web page, you can resize even smaller. An image measuring just 150 pixels across may give a satisfactory preview of the larger image.

Apart from resizing images, you may also want a lower quality setting for JPEG compression—to minimize the download time for your photos. Some programs give a preview of what the image will look like after going through higher compression to reduce file size. Others, like Picasa (pictured right), might allow you to change size and quality at the same time.

Online Photo Hosting

You don't have to swamp your loved ones' e-mail accounts with image file attachments. Several Internet hosting sites cater to photographers who want to set up a photo Web page without hassle. Others can then view your photos at their leisure.

▶ ▶ ▶ PBase.com

With over 60,000 photo galleries and millions of photos, PBase is one of the popular photo hosting sites. Trial accounts may be created for up to 30 days, but you will need to pay for a permanent account. PBase supports hot linking; this means that you can make your pictures from PBase appear on other Web pages and forums.

You can design the look of your gallery yourself or just use one of the standard ones provided.

▲ Gallery design and images from PBase.com

▶ ▶ ▶ flickr.com

On this hosting site, you can create accounts for free, but there are limitations on the number of megabytes that can be uploaded per month and the number of photos you can display. You can also have a paid account, for increased capacities.

▶ ▶ ▶ PhotoSite.com

This site offers both free and paid accounts. A free account limits you to 150 photos. However, PhotoSite offers a wide range of backgrounds and frames to give your photos an attractive layout easily.

▲ Screenshot from flickr.com
Reproduced with permission of Yahoo! Inc.
©2006 Yahoo! Inc. YAHOO! and the YAHOO! logo are the trademark of Yahoo! Inc.

▶ ▶ ▶ Kodak EasyShare Gallery

This site hosts photos as well, but requires you to purchase prints of your photos to maintain the free hosting. Services are mainly for the USA and a few European countries.

▶ ▶ ▶ Other Options

There are other photo hosting sites besides these. Alternatively, some photographers share photos by putting them on their weblogs, such as those hosted by Blogger. If you have your own Web site, you can also share your photos by uploading them.

30

Printing Considerations

Images viewed on screen may look good because they are illuminated, but to many people, there is nothing better than an actual print for real enjoyment of a photograph. We will now look at some options and considerations in preparing your photos for output.

Doing the Resolution Math

There are four variables involved in printing calculations: sensor resolution, image resolution, print size, and printer resolution. Basically, you should first set the print size, then check the image resolution.

- **Sensor resolution**: As mentioned previously, this is equivalent to the pixel dimensions or pixel count of the image. It is measured in pixels; for example, a sensor resolution of 3008 × 2000 pixels equals about 6 megapixels total.

- **Image resolution**: This specifies how closely the pixels are spaced, and is usually measured in pixels per inch, or ppi. For inkjet printing, settings of at least 200 to 300 ppi are required for the human eye to perceive that there is no visible pixelation (i.e., a jagged, "digital" appearance) in the print. Some printers work better with specific image resolutions, such as 240 or 272 ppi. Check your printer documentation to find your optimal setting.

- **Print size**: Dividing sensor resolution by print size calculates the image resolution. For example, if the sensor has a vertical resolution of 2000 pixels, and your print size measures 4" high, the resulting ppi is 500. The ppi of any image can be changed with an editing program independently of the print size, but this requires adding or subtracting pixel data, and can reduce the quality of your final image.

Editing programs like the GIMP (http://www.gimp.org) allow you to adjust these variables at the same time. If you change either of the settings, the other will adjust automatically. Here the original image has been downsized to 1444 × 960 pixels. This will produce a 6" × 4" photo at exactly 240 ppi.

- **Printer Resolution:** This depends on the printer model. Printers are limited by how many separate ink dots per inch, or dpi, they can accurately print. This is different from the number of pixels per inch. A printer at 1440 dpi, printing a 240 ppi image, will print approximately 6 ink dots along the width of each pixel. High-resolution printing —such as 1440 dpi— should be able to render smooth areas of tone and precise colors, without the appearance of color banding or pixelation. Generally, printer resolution must match, if not exceed, image resolution.

You will need to do some test printing at different dpi settings to find your printer's optimum setting. Some have found that their printers deliver the best results at 600 dpi. Others may find optimal results at 1440 dpi. It depends on the design of each printer.

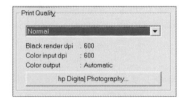

Printing Options

▶ ▶ ▶ Inkjet Printers

Inkjet printers are relatively affordable and give good image quality. Most can print A4 (8.27" × 11.69") or letter (8.5" × 11") size photos. More expensive models can print A3 (16.53" × 11.69") size photos. Newer photo-quality inkjet printers are designed to print with six or more different ink colors. Generally, more ink colors means better rendering of colors and tones in your images.

The lifespan of an inkjet print depends on the exact combination of ink and paper used. Inkjet prints have had a reputation for fading after a few years or even months, especially if exposed to sunlight. Things have been improving, but for best results, archival-quality inks and papers have been developed. When the right ink-paper combination is used, you get much better print longevity.

▶ ▶ ▶ Dye Sublimation Printers

These printers apply dyes to paper, instead of ink droplets. Whereas inkjets use fine droplets to give the appearance of continuous tone, dye-sub printers are actually able to print continuous tones, giving dye-sub prints excellent photo quality. Unfortunately, many dye-sub printers only produce small prints (e.g., 6" × 4"). Printers for larger formats are considerably more expensive than comparable inkjets.

▶ ▶ ▶ Commercial Photofinishing

If you want prints that last longer than the standard inkjet print, but do not wish to spend more money on better equipment, or if you want many prints in a short period of time, you can visit a photofinishing shop with your photos on a CD or memory card. Digital photo labs generally use commercial printing machines, giving you photo quality similar to commercial prints from film. Some of these machines have lower ppi requirements than inkjets, allowing you to get larger prints made.

Some shops have self-service kiosks that allow you to select the size and the number of copies to be printed. Some machines even allow for simple image enhancement.

Other labs process your files the same way they process negatives—adjusting color and contrast on their machines. This can work for you or against you. If the staff is skilled, you may not need to do much image editing after taking photos, as the shop will do a decent job for you. On the other hand, if you have spent time fine-tuning your photos in Photoshop, you will probably not want the shop staff to adjust or "undo" your careful editing.

▶ ▶ ▶ Online Printing

Ordering prints from the Internet is easy, even if the prices aren't the cheapest. You may need to download software from the online service's site in order to upload your photos to the company's server. You'll then likely have the option of receiving your prints via mail or picking them up at a local store. In any case, this is often a great way to streamline the printing process when you really need professional prints.

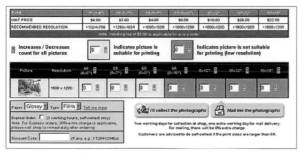

▲ fujifilm.com.sg

40 Digital SLR Techniques

Maximizing Your RAW Potential

The processing speeds and large memory buffers of DSLRs make shooting in the RAW image format a viable option (many compact digital cameras cannot do this speedily, if at all). The RAW format offers you maximum flexibility and quality in editing your photos. Apart from allowing the use of detachable lenses, RAW capability is one of the strongest arguments in favor of using a DSLR camera.

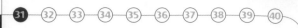

31

What Is RAW?

A RAW file is the complete, unprocessed digital signal captured by your DSLR's imaging sensor. Pure luminance (brightness) values from each pixel are recorded, unaffected by interpolation or processing parameters. Choices made (such as sharpening and white balance) merely accompany the raw data—they do not alter it. In other words, RAW files are "uncooked," and this gives you the greatest control from start to finish.

Advantages of the RAW Format

● **Bit depth:** DSLRs currently use 12- or 14-bit analog-digital conversion. So you get 2^{12} (more than 4,000) or 2^{14} (over 16,000) distinct tonal levels to work with, compared with only 2^8 (or 256) levels for camera-produced JPEGs or TIFFs. Using software such as Adobe Photoshop allows you to work in 16-bit mode to take advantage of higher bit depth. You'll get better tonal gradations and highlight/shadow details as a result.

▲ This original JPEG has blown highlights. ▲ Most of the image can be restored from RAW.

● **Adjustable processing:** Instead of relying on your camera's processing at the point of capture, you can apply parameters such as white balance, sharpening, contrast, and noise reduction to the raw image data. You can also use specialized software that gives results superior to those from the camera.

- **Lossless format:** No image data is lost through file compression, so your photos are "pure." You can maintain this through the entire processing stage, and possibly through to printing stage.
- **Better resizing:** Resizing and resolution adjustments can be handled simultaneously, so you may get better detail in resized images.
- **Simultaneous JPEG capture:** Some cameras can save two versions of each file, one in RAW and another in the JPEG format. If your DSLR can save RAW plus a high-quality JPEG, you can simply use the JPEG if the image turns out right. This allows for greater freedom and control over your image files.
- **Future improvements:** If better processing methods or tools are developed, you will be able to benefit by running your RAW images through them. You might potentially get better images than what today's cameras and computers can produce.

Disadvantages of the RAW Format

- **Lower shooting rate:** Because all the sensor data is saved losslessly to your memory card, the camera's processing engine and buffer slow down due to the sheer amount of information. Memory cards fill up much faster, too. This is one reason why action shots are usually captured in JPEG format.
- **"Incomplete" state:** Unless others have the software to view your RAW files directly, you can only share your images after you have processed them. For high-volume work or short deadlines, the need to process and/or transmit pictures can exclude the RAW format from consideration.
- **Computer processing and storage:** RAW images require more powerful computers for processing. They also take more space when archived on hard disk or CD/DVD media.
- **Skill and effort required:** A DSLR usually produces JPEG files of high quality, almost instantaneously. Although 8-bit and compressed, good JPEGs can be nearly indistinguishable from RAW images. Shooting in RAW presupposes that you will be able to produce better results on your computer, but this isn't always true.
- **Proprietary formats:** To call RAW a "format" can be misleading. Each manufacturer develops and patents their own RAW formats, which can even vary between models. If support for any camera's RAW files is discontinued, they face the danger of being rendered useless.

Sample Comparison

Here are two images from a simultaneous RAW+JPEG capture. They have been processed in Adobe Photoshop to give a rich, saturated color. On a computer, their histograms can be displayed, and you can see that the image converted from RAW to JPEG has a smoother histogram than the directly captured JPEG.

▲ JPEG converted from RAW   ▲ Manipulated camera JPEG

◄ The detail and color are also better in the RAW version.

Conclusion

Basically, the main advantage of RAW formats is their superior quality and flexibility. If you want the very highest quality and are prepared to put in the necessary time and effort, RAW will suit you. The main reason to shoot in JPEG is speed and instant access. If time is of the essence, you will most likely find your camera's processing quality sufficient for your needs.

32 RAW Viewers and Converters

The first step in a RAW workflow is organizing and selecting images for editing. Use a RAW file viewer to preview and make initial decisions. Then, use a RAW converter to process the raw data into a digital photo ready for image editing.

Proprietary vs. Third—Party Software

Camera manufacturers develop their own software to view and convert RAW images. Some people think that the manufacturer possesses the best knowledge of their own RAW format, so proprietary software would be the best option.

Some makers produce a range of software. For example, Nikon camera users have two free viewers and editors to choose from: Nikon View and PictureProject (which merely has a nicer interface). Both programs are not fully featured; you will need to purchase Nikon Capture for proper control over RAW conversion.

Since some expenditure on software is unavoidable, photographers are likely to consider third-party options rather than proprietary programs–to ensure maximum functionality. BreezeBrowser (http://www.breezesys.com) and Capture One DSLR (http://www.phaseone.com) are independent programs for RAW viewing and conversion. One free RAW converter worth trying out is RawShooter Essentials (http://www.pixmantec.com).

For a total solution, many serious photographers invest in the full-featured (but expensive) Adobe Photoshop (http://www.adobe.com) software suite, as its file viewer, RAW converter, and image editing functions all work together seamlessly. We will examine the Adobe Bridge viewer on the next page.

Adobe Bridge

Adobe Bridge (http://www.adobe.com) acts as a hub for various media files and programs. Once installed, open the program and navigate to your image folder on the hard disk. At the bottom-right corner, you can choose between thumbnail view (with selectable viewing size) and three kinds of single-image view.

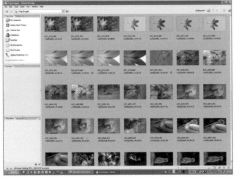

▲ Thumbnail view

▲ Strip view

When you view RAW images, they are first displayed using the camera's parameters. You can even use Adobe Bridge to copy Adobe Camera RAW (Adobe's RAW image editing program) settings from one image and apply them to other images, as a simple way to use the same settings. If you later adjust the parameters in Adobe Camera RAW, the adjustments will be reflected when viewing the image in Adobe Bridge.

You can also view EXIF data showing your camera settings. Either choose the single-image view with information, or use the bottom-left info box, which shows details for the currently selected image.

When you have selected RAW images to convert, open them in Camera RAW. (Read the next technique to get acquainted with this program.)

33

Adobe Camera RAW—Basic Parameters

With RAW files and a RAW converter, you need not worry about setting the white balance or contrast incorrectly. A program like Adobe Camera RAW gives you the flexibility of experimenting with all the settings to produce several versions of the same shot, all with the same quality as an original image from your camera.

The Camera RAW Window

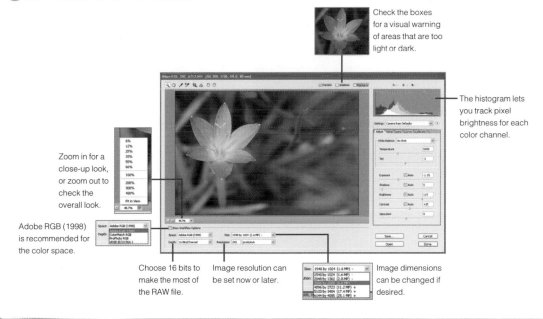

Check the boxes for a visual warning of areas that are too light or dark.

The histogram lets you track pixel brightness for each color channel.

Zoom in for a close-up look, or zoom out to check the overall look.

Adobe RGB (1998) is recommended for the color space.

Choose 16 bits to make the most of the RAW file.

Image resolution can be set now or later.

Image dimensions can be changed if desired.

Basic Parameter Settings

Work
your way
down the
options.

❶ Color temperature (white balance).

▲ Too cool   ▲ Too warm

❷ Tint: Useful for subtle color shifts and indoor lighting.

❸ Exposure: Avoid letting the histogram touch the left and right edges.

❹ Shadow: Focuses on the darker regions.

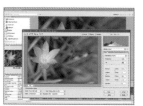

▲ Low

▲ Too dark

▲ Too much (shadow warning)

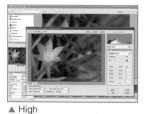

▲ High

▲ Too bright (highlight warning)

▲ Too little

Adjust the sliders to see the effects they produce. As you get a feel for each setting, make increasingly finer adjustments until you get the results you want.

You do not have to adjust the settings in the order shown here. The parameters interact in a complex way; so you may have to go back and fine-tune earlier settings as you progress.

If you don't like the results, you can always reset the values to their default settings. Camera RAW does not change the RAW file itself; your settings are saved in a separate file that Camera RAW references.

❺ Brightness: Tune the whole image.

❻ Contrast.

❼ Saturation: Adjust the overall color intensity.

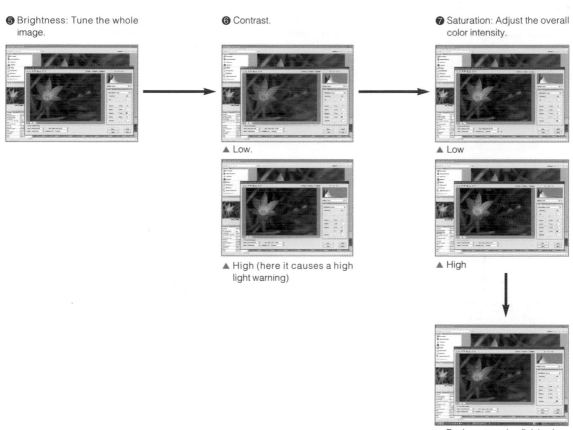

▲ Low.

▲ Low

▲ High (here it causes a high light warning)

▲ High

▲ Basic processing finished

34

Adobe Camera RAW— Advanced Parameters

Camera RAW has many advanced controls for the expert user. We will look at one more set of controls here: the options on the Detail tab at the right side of the Camera RAW window, just below the histogram. Here, you can adjust basic settings for sharpening lines and details, as well as smoothening of unwanted noise.

Sharpening and Noise Reduction

The Detail section of Camera RAW has just three settings. Before you adjust the sliders, first set the zoom to 100% to see the image pixel-for-pixel on your monitor.

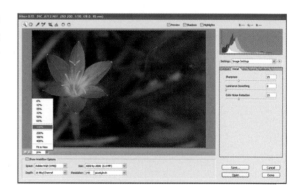

Chapter 6

▶ ▶ ▶ Sharpness

This setting controls the crispness of the edges in the photo. If you are going to manipulate the image further in Photoshop, you may want to avoid a high setting, leaving the sharpening for the last step in your editing process.

 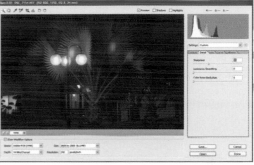

▲ The original image is shown on the left. On the right, even a moderate sharpness setting makes the lamps pop out of the picture.

▶ ▶ ▶ Luminance Smoothing

Digital noise can form the appearance of uneven texture, caused by pixels of varying brightness. Luminance smoothing evens out textures to make them appear more natural, but too high a setting may cause actual image details to be reduced.

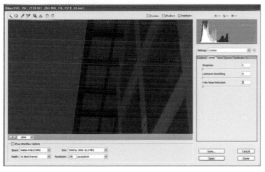 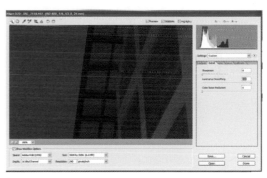

▲ On the right, you can see the smoothening effect a high setting has.

▶ ▶ ▶ Color Noise Reduction

Very often, digital noise occurs as pixels of random colors, giving shadow areas in particular a speckled appearance. This setting attempts to reduce such color noise.

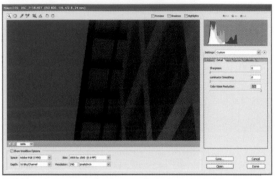

▲ With color noise reduction applied, there is visible texture on the walls, but it is of even color.

In the next section, we will take a brief look at noise reduction software. If you plan on using such programs, use conservative settings for both luminance smoothing and color noise reduction, and let the specialized software do the job.

35

Noise Management

Most people find digital noise unpleasant, sometimes more than they would traditional film grain. Fortunately, digital photographers have a number of software tools at their disposal, delivering superb noise reduction capabilities.

Software Options

Users generally have a choice between standalone programs or plug-ins. A standalone program is run on its own; it may offer batch processing for greater efficiency. On the other hand, plug-ins are designed to work with software such as Adobe Photoshop. They are activated from within the host program, and are therefore easy to integrate into the editing workflow.

Some noteworthy noise reduction programs include Neat Image (http://www.neatimage.com), Imagenomic's Noiseware (http://www.imagenomic.com), PictureCode's Noise Ninja (http://www.picturecode.com), and Visual Infinity's Grain Surgery (http://www.visinf.com). As an example for this section, we will use Noise Ninja's Photoshop plug-in.

See the image to the right. Notice that the white cloth and the skin are mottled with color noise.

From the Filters menu, run Noise Ninja. The first screen is for profiling. By selecting areas of even overall brightness, you give the software some idea of your camera's noise "profile." It will attempt to remove noise of a similar pattern throughout the entire image. You should choose sample areas from highlight, mid-tone, and shadow regions if possible.

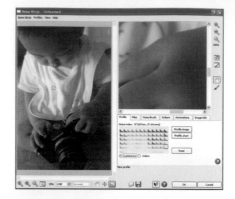

Now, go to the next tab. There are three main adjustments, which are made using sliders. Noise Ninja recommends setting the strength to maximum, then adjusting smoothness to the minimum setting that is acceptable.

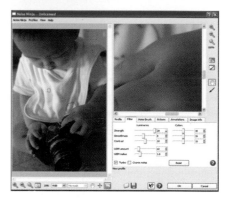

The next step will be to reduce the strength filter to a minimum level.

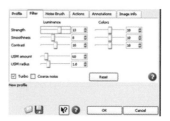

Noise Ninja offers sharpening using Unsharp Masking (USM). You can apply USM at this stage, or leave it for last using Photoshop's own USM. Use the Hand tool to move the image around, checking that details in various parts of the picture are acceptably rendered.

Move the image around to lighter and darker regions, checking the balance between noise reduction and retention of image detail.

In a nutshell, the noise reduction capabilities of Noise Ninja and similar products are impressive. While care must be taken not to overdo image smoothening, you can be certain that digital noise will hardly be a problem with such tools at hand.

40 Digital SLR Techniques

Editing in Adobe Photoshop CS2

Adobe Photoshop has established itself as the industry standard for image editing software. While there are hundreds of ways you can modify and enhance your photos, there are a few basic steps that most photographers will find useful. In this chapter, we will start off with a look at working with color, and proceed to outline some simple procedures for tone and color adjustments, using the latest version of Photoshop.

Chapter 7

36

Color Spaces and Calibration

The same digital photo can look different depending on whether it is viewed on the camera's LCD or on a computer monitor. When printed out, the image can again appear to have changed in brightness or contrast. To avoid such inconsistencies and get the best results, your workflow has to include basic color management.

Color Spaces

A digital camera converts light into digital color data. A monitor converts the data into an illuminated image on screen, while printers convert the data into a print, using the inks specified by the software. The way these devices handle digital information depends on their makers' interpretation of the data, as well as the exact technology used. Needless to say, devices vary in the way they reproduce color.

A color space is a mathematically mapped set of colors that can be defined by variables. The most common type of color space for digital cameras is RGB. An RGB color space defines the colors that can be produced by combining Red, Green, and Blue values. There are a few RGB color spaces, of which sRGB and Adobe RGB are the most well-known.

Many digital cameras, monitors, and printers conform to the sRGB color space, enabling reasonably consistent color representation from device to device. The gamut of sRGB, however, is rather small; the total range of possible colors is limited.

The Adobe RGB color space has a wider gamut, allowing a greater range of colors to be represented. If you shoot images in Adobe RGB, however, you have to adjust your computer and printer to use the same color space, or else colors will not be reproduced correctly. Some people choose to edit images in Adobe RGB to make use of the wider color space it offers, and at the end convert to the smaller-gamut sRGB for output to devices, such as printers, that do not support other color spaces.

Printing presses use a different color model (i.e., colors are defined by different variables). Four-color printing uses the CMYK model, comprising Cyan, Magenta, Yellow, and blacK intensities. The related color spaces, and their gamuts, can be quite different.

Photoshop gives you the ability to work in specified color spaces, and to convert between color spaces.

Setting Color Space in Adobe Photoshop

In Photoshop, go to Edit > Color Settings to set color spaces.

Under Working Spaces, you can select Adobe RGB (1998) to use this color space. This is particularly useful if you want a wider gamut when working with RAW files.

Under Color Management Policies, set Preserve Embedded Profiles, and check the Profile Mismatches options. This way, you can keep an eye on varying color settings. When editing sRGB images, you have the option to work in sRGB, or convert the image to the Adobe RGB color space.

For Conversion Options, use the Adobe (ACE) engine and set Intent to Perceptual. Both options can be checked.

The Description box at the bottom gives you more information on the various options. When you are done with the settings, you can save them.

Monitor Calibration Using Adobe Gamma

Now that you have set your color options, you should calibrate your monitor. Having the right settings is no use if your monitor does not display colors correctly, as any adjustments you make won't be accurately represented on the screen. Various utility programs are available, but we will use Adobe Gamma as an example, since it is installed when you install Photoshop.

Let your monitor stay on for an hour, so that the display stabilizes. In the Windows Control Panel, open Adobe Gamma. (Mac users will find a somewhat similar set of adjustments in their Displays control panel.)

▲ Choose the Step By Step (Wizard) and follow the instructions.

▲ If you have a monitor profile (monitor settings saved as a file), you can load it.

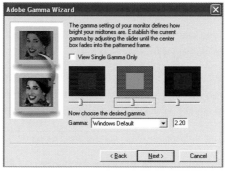

▲ The steps shown above adjust the brightness and contrast so that tones will be shown in correct relationship to each other.

When adjusting gamma, uncheck the View Single Gamma Only option to see one box for each color. Adjust each slider until the individual colors are adjusted properly. You may find it helpful to look at the boxes with slightly unfocused vision and at different distances.

For the other settings, check your hardware documentation, or use the suggested settings. After you are done, save the new calibrated monitor profile, preferably with the date in the filename. This is useful because monitor performance can change over time.

Now that you have defined your working color spaces and calibrated your monitor, you should be able to see and adjust image color on screen more accurately.

Hardware Calibration

Some users may require critical color matching, such as when doing product photography. For more precise calibration, you can purchase a hardware and software package. Examples are ColorVision's Spyder2 and X-Rite's MonacoOPTIX. When attached to the face of the monitor, the calibration device can set up the display much more accurately.

▲ ColorVision Spyder2

37

Converting Color Modes and Spaces

Adobe Photoshop enables you to import your digital images, convert them to a color space for editing, and then output them to a different color space or color model for printing or online viewing. Changing between these options is handled without fuss by the program.

Changing Modes

When editing your pictures, you might need to manipulate colors in different ways.

In the screenshot to the right, the image is made up of the standard RGB channels. Select Image > Mode to change from RGB to other color modes.

The image here has been changed to CMYK mode. Now there are four channels visible beneath the composite channel.

Clicking off the visibility of the cyan and magenta channels shows the yellow and black channels. This illustrates the distinct difference between this and the usual RGB mode.

On the right, the image has been changed to Lab mode (consisting of Lightness, plus A and B channels). Among other things, this mode can be useful for black-and-white conversion, as well as sharpening the image (see the following sections).

Converting Color Space

If you wish to permanently convert images from one color space to another (e.g., from Adobe RGB to sRGB), choose Edit > Convert to Profile to do so. This does more than change modes; it is a final step in preparing files for output, whether to printer or screen.

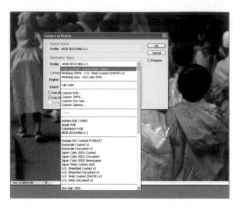

Soft Proofing

Even though many devices use the sRGB color space, they still vary in the exact colors they can reproduce, often due to the way they work, and their design. Even the same printer will produce different results depending on the specific inks and paper used.

Some manufacturers therefore make color profiles available for their products. Color profiles are useful because they describe the way a device handles color within the color space. A printer can have a generic profile, or it can have separate profiles for specific ink-paper combinations.

Photoshop has soft-proofing capability; in other words, it can simulate how an image would appear if printed to a particular device (or type of device), either a printer or a monitor. If you are preparing images for press, you can select generic CMYK proofing. If you have a specific output profile, you need to install it in Photoshop first.

Select View > Proof Setup to view the options. For installed profiles, select Custom. Otherwise, choose an option.

The screenshots show the same image, as-is (left) and as simulated CMYK (right).

Since the image does look as if it would be more dull if printed in CMYK, you can stay in proof view while doing final color adjustments for press. This way, you will be more likely to have the right colors for the final output.

38 Levels and Curves

Many photographers simply want to perform basic enhancement of color, brightness, and contrast on their photos. The Levels and Curves tools should be sufficient for most adjustments. For best results, do image corrections only after setting up basic color management as described in the preceding sections.

Levels

Each pixel in an RGB image is composed of three channels. Each channel has a certain brightness level. Combined, the values determine the pixel's color. At the lowest end, a pixel with (R:0, G:0, B:0) would be totally black. At the opposite end (for 8-bit images), a pixel with (R:255, G: 255, B:255) would be pure white.

The Levels tool lets you change brightness and contrast by modifying the relationships between the different tonal levels of an image. Click Layer > New Adjustment Layer > Levels to begin.

Moving the white point slider to the left brightens the image. Pixels to the right of the slider reach maximum brightness; highlight detail may be lost.

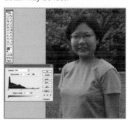

The histogram shows the distribution of pixels, arranged with darkest at left and brightest on the right.

Moving the black point slider to the right darkens the image. Pixels to the left of the slider become pure black; shadow detail may be lost.

The mid-point slider adjusts the mid-tones. Pixels to the left become the darker tones; those to the right end up as lighter tones.

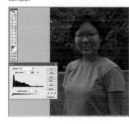

You may notice that moving a slider mostly changes the levels closest to the slider position, but it does affect the rest of the image.

For the final image to the right, the white and mid-point sliders were adjusted to lift the mid-tones a bit, while maintaining good contrast.

▶ ▶ ▶ Basic Levels Workflow

Now that you have an idea of how the sliders function, let's go through another Levels adjustment step by step. Note that this is just one possible way to adjust levels.

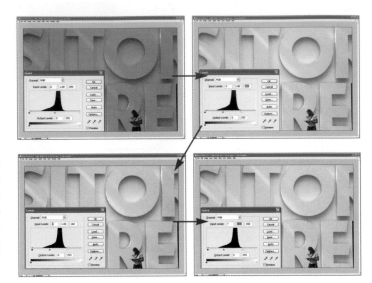

On opening the image, the histogram displays quite a bit of unused space on the left and right. The first thing to do is to move the white point in till the slider touches the very tip of where the pixels begin. The wall now looks white, as it should.

Next, the black point is moved in till it just touches the small bump which represents the little bit of door frame visible in the picture. Last, the mid-point is adjusted to restore proper brightness to the lone figure. This simple adjustment has made a significant improvement to the image.

Curves

The Curves tool is a more sophisticated tool. It allows you to do adjustments similar to Levels, but also gives you control over specific tones without affecting the rest of the image, if you so choose.

Choose Create Layer > New Adjustment Layer > Curves to bring up the Curves window. The curve is the black line running from the bottom left to the top right of the square box. Along the bottom, the horizontal black-to-white gradient represents the tonal range of the original image—the input. Along the left-hand side, the vertical gradient represents the output tonal range. The relationship between the input and output tones is controlled by the shape of the curve. You can think of it as changing the

X-Y correlation between them. It is not easy to visualize, so experimenting with the Curves tool will be a more practical way to find out just what it does.

Clicking on the curve creates a control point. You can create several points to keep your curve fixed at set points.

You can use the Eyedropper tool to find out where different parts of your picture are located on the curve. When you click on one spot in the image, the relevant part of the curve is pinpointed by a small circle. This way, you can be more precise as to which part of the curve needs adjustment.

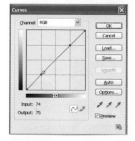

Generally, add control points when the existing ones are not sufficient to give the effect you want. You can delete extra control points. Drag the points around until you get the effect you are seeking.

The screenshot to the right shows the large adjustment needed to brighten the mid-tones. The commuters (actually a reflection in the window) and the apartment lights outside are now more visible. The challenge was to reveal these details without making the carriage too visible. To do this, the top-right corner of the curve was brought a bit lower.

Sample-Based Adjustment to Levels and Curves

Instead of going through the hassle of adjusting sliders or control point, you can also use the sampling eyedroppers in the Levels and Curves dialog boxes. Pick white, black, and (if possible) gray points in your photo, and Photoshop will attempt to adjust the colors accordingly. This approach requires the presence of neutral sample points.

Adjusting Individual Colors

So far, we have looked at overall levels and curves that affect the entire image. You can also adjust these parameters for the individual color channels. This enables precise color correction or enhancement.

To illustrate single-channel adjustments, here are screenshots from the GIMP (http://www.gimp.org), which uses levels and curve controls similar to Photoshop's, but includes a histogram which here shows a tall spike at left, representing the black background. Note that only the green channel is selected.

Adding green in the shoulder of the curve; the lighter crayons are tinted green.

Reducing green in the shoulder of the curve; the lighter crayons are tinted magenta.

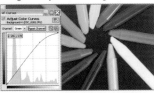
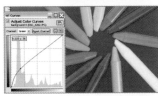

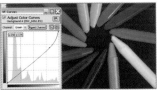
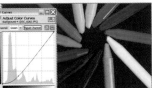

Adding green in the toe of the curve; the darker crayons and background are tinted green.

Reducing green in the toe of the curve; the darker crayons and background are tinted magenta.

An S-curve increases green contrast and gives vivid greens, but a magenta cast in the dark tones.

A reverse S-curve decreases green contrast; very flat greens, and a magenta cast in the light tones.

The chart below summarizes some basic color relationships. Reducing values in an RGB channel will increase the intensity of the opposite color. Alternatively, you could adjust the other two channels.

Channel adjusted	Opposite color (formed by the other two channels)
Red	Cyan (Green + Blue)
Green	Magenta (Red + Blue)
Blue	Yellow (Red + Green)

39 Black-and-White Conversion

Fans of black-and-white photography may worry that the DSLR makes it difficult to get B+W images. Quite a few cameras capture images exclusively in color, necessitating conversion to B+W using a computer. Although some DSLRs have a black-and-white capture mode, this may not give results quite like traditional B+W film; such images also cannot be converted to color. In this section, we'll cover the various methods for converting to black-and-white in Photoshop.

Grayscale

The simplest way to convert to B+W is to select Image > Mode > Grayscale. The results can look rather flat, though.

Russell Preston Brown Tonal Conversion Technique

This more advanced technique by Photoshop guru Russell Brown uses two hue and saturation layers instead of a single Hue/Saturation adjustment. Create Layer > New Adjustment Layer > Hue/Saturation twice. For the top layer, set Saturation to -100, similar to above. For the layer below, set blending mode to Color. Then adjust Hue and Lightness for the whole image or selected colour ranges, similar to above.

⒟esaturate

By using a Hue/Saturation adjustment, you can adjust Saturation to -100, which is the same as the grayscale action above, but you can also adjust the Lightness setting for a little more control.

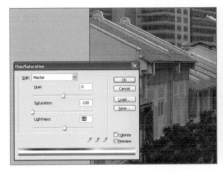 

For more tweaking, you can adjust Hue and Lightness for the whole image or for selected colors to alter the tonal relationships. The bars at the bottom show how you are altering the original color values.

Lab Mode

This is almost as quick as a grayscale conversion, but gives generally nicer results. Go to Image > Mode > Lab Color. Select only the Lightness channel, and either discard the rest or select Image > Mode > Grayscale.

Channel Mixer

This is the standard B+W conversion method. Before beginning, you can view each color channel singly to get a hint as to how to start.

The red channel (on the left in the images shown on the previous page) is the most noisy, and the skin tones are similar to the shirts. The green channel (middle) is quite good; you could delete the other two and just use this (similar to Lab conversion). The blue channel (right) gives contrast on the chessboard, but makes the left-most face too dark. The green channel seems to be the best starting point.

Select Layer > New Adjustment Layer > Channel Mixer. You can adjust the sliders or type values in the boxes. Make sure Monochrome is checked, and try to make the three channel values add up to 100. In the screenshot to the upper right, the preview image has 68% of the green channel and 36% of the blue.

Last, some red values have been added to lighten the skin tones. The mix is +42% red, +52% green, and +14% blue. The final result is better than the other methods we've covered so far.

Toning Effects

While Photoshop doesn't exactly give the same results as traditional B+W chemistry, you can duplicate the effects of toning using sepia, gold, or selenium, without having to handle toxic chemicals. First, change the photo to Image > Mode > Grayscale. Then, select Image > Mode > Duotone.

In the Duotone Options pop-up, if you select Duotone as the Type, you can click the Ink 2 color box to select from a wide range of colors. Tritone and Quadtone use three and four inks, respectively.

Whichever toning option you select, you are also given the option of adjusting the curves for each ink. Click the little curve box next to each ink color to adjust how much ink should be applied to the different tonal levels of the image. When you are done, choose Image > Mode > RGB so that you can save the image as a normal TIFF or JPEG.

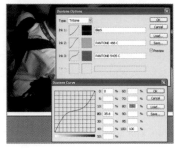

Further Adjustments

In traditional B+W, you had to think ahead when beginning to make a print, because subsequent treatments such as toning or bleaching would change the image density. In the digital darkroom, this is less of a concern. Using Photoshop's layers and history, you can alter your settings at any stage, without degrading the final image.

You can easily add a levels or curves layer to enhance your B+W image, especially after changing to Duotone mode. In the example shown here, the screenshot at left shows the results of using the Channel Mixer. The histogram has no values at the right end. Adjusting the white point with Levels decidedly improves the tonal distribution for more tonal punch.

Sharpening Images

Software sharpening is a given in digital imaging. If you are printing straight from the camera, you could probably rely on the built-in sharpening algorithm to do the work for you. But if you want better quality, you should reduce or deactivate in-camera sharpening and use the Unsharp Mask (USM) filter instead.

USM: Function and Workflow

In digital sharpening, the computer locates edges (defined by a difference in contrast) and draws outlines (bright or dark lines) along these edges. This gives the impression of greater sharpness along edges. Unfortunately, because of the way it works, sharpening cannot rescue unfocused photos—they have no edges to outline.

Sharpening is often the last step in image editing, carried out before the final save. There are a few good reasons for this. First, the amount of sharpening you need depends on the how you use the final image. Printing to different sizes, and different on-screen magnifications, will all require different amounts of sharpening. Second, effective sharpening settings depend on the nature of the subject matter. Fine detail in landscapes is not the same as the clean lines of modern architecture. Visible skin texture is more expected in portraits of men, perhaps. Additionally, editing an image after sharpening also alters the sharpening outlines, possibly creating ugly or artificial results.

On the other hand, judicious sharpening after other adjustments have been completed—especially resizing of image dimensions—can bring out the detail in a photo and enhance its appearance. Photoshop's Unsharp Mask filter is the most popular tool for sharpening, although third-party plug-ins are also available. You can also explore the Smart Sharpen filter, which enables selective sharpening and reduction of motion blur.

USM Settings

To correctly gauge the effects of sharpening, first view the image at 100%. Then, activate Filter > Sharpen > Unsharp Mask. A window pops up, with three settings adjusted either by sliders or keyed values.

These three variables interact with each other, so you may need to move back and forth, fine-tuning them in relation to each other.

You should also be aware that the final judgment for print sharpening is an actual test print. You will need to experiment with both your sharpening and print settings to find out what works well.

▶ ▶ ▶ Amount

This setting determines how visible the sharpening effect is. Generally, begin by trying values of 100-200%.

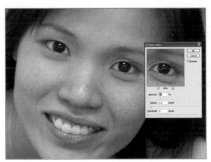

▲ 44%: hardly any visible effect

▲ 200%: skin texture looks coarse

▶ ▶ ▶ Radius

The radius refers to the width of the outlines drawn within and outside edges. Values of a few pixels are used; a common starting point is to divide the output resolution by 200. You can adjust in 0.1 pixel increments.

▲ 0.9 pixels: very slight effect

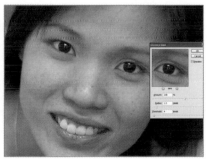

▲ 1.8 pixels: obvious sharpening

▶ ▶ ▶ Threshold

The Threshold value sets the minimum difference in contrast that is needed for USM to recognize something as an edge to be sharpened. Low settings result in most edges being sharpened; higher settings mean that only more obvious edges will be sharpened. This affords you some control over which parts of the image are sharpened.

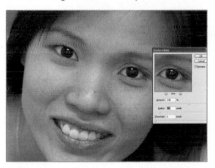

▲ 0 levels: whole image sharpened, including pores on skin

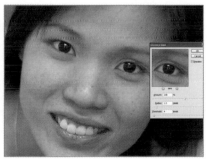

▲ 4 levels: most skin not sharpened, overall smoother effect

Striking a Balance

For this photo of a crowned crane, an Amount of 190%, Radius 3.2 pixels, and Threshold of 8 levels was first applied. This shows the effect of a Radius setting that is obviously too high: a halo is visible around the neck and the feathers around the head.

The settings were then adjusted to a Radius of 1.0 and a Threshold of 0. This effect is better, but it also shows that the low threshold sharpens the whole image. The background especially becomes grainy or noisy.

Finally, the version here uses a higher Amount of 216%, together with a Radius of 1.0 and the original Threshold of 8. It achieves a compromise between sharpening the crane and keeping the overall noise levels low.

Other Approaches to Sharpening

So far the examples have discussed sharpening of the whole image. Some other techniques may give better results, especially for images that are difficult to sharpen normally.

- **Feathered selections**: Instead of sharpening the whole image, you can use the Marquee tool to select specific areas for sharpening. Different areas of the picture can then be sharpened differently. Feather the selections to avoid noticeable transitions between areas.

- **Selected RGB channels**: Instead of sharpening all channels, sharpen just one or two, possibly the ones showing most of the areas that need sharpening, or the ones that have the least noise.

- **Lab Lightness channel**: This is similar to the method above, except that the mode is changed from RGB to Lab. Since color noise is sometimes a problem in digital photos, removing color information from the sharpening stage may help keep noise levels down. Also, the human eye is more sensitive to shapes as defined by different tones, rather than by colors. This further supports the choice to sharpen Lightness only.

It takes time and patience to become competent at sharpening, as well as other aspects of digital image editing. Above all, be willing to learn from others and try things out for yourself. With your DSLR and software such as Photoshop CS2, you can have the satisfaction of being involved in the entire picture-making process: from camera capture through to the finished product.

Index

Acknowledgements

The credits for the images displayed in *40 Digital SLR Techniques* are as follows. We would also like to take this opportunity to thank the author for providing the images.

Images in this book may not be copied and/or duplicated without the written consent of the copyright holder.

Photo © 2006   D. Tan (except Bayer & Foveon image): 1-65
Photo © 2006   D. Tan (except some product images): 66-111
Photo © 2006   Lak Yau: 114
Photo © 2006   Eu Lee: 115-117
Photo © 2006   D. Tan: 118
Photo © 2006   Eu Lee: 119-121
Photo © 2006   D. Tan: 122-127
Photo © 2006   Rand Miranda: 128 top
Photo © 2006   Eu Lee: 128-133
Photo © 2006   D. Tan: 138-148
Photo © 2006   Cheah Weng Kwong and D. Tan: 150-158
Photo © 2006   D. Tan: 159-162
Photo © 2006   Lak Yau: 163 top
Photo © 2006   D. Tan: 163-167
Photo © 2006   Paul Tan Hsien Loong: 168-175
Photo © 2006   D. Tan (except some product images): 176-211
Photo © 2006   D. Tan (except some product images): 212-235

All product images within this book are copyrighted by their corresponding companies.

page 11 Image used with permission of Foveon X3® Image Sensor © 2003 Foveon, Inc.
pages 56 and 57 Matrix and spot metering pattern images used with permission of Fuji Photo Film U.S.A., Inc.
page 92 Photo used with permission of LumiQuest®.
page 94 Photo used with permission of Visual Echoes.
page 151 Photo used with permission of Wimberly, Inc.
page 187 Photo used with permission of Verbatim Corporation, Inc.